The Italic Way to Beautiful Handwriting

Cursive & Calligraphic

Fred Eager

Macmillan Publishing Co., Inc.
NEW YORK

Macmillan Publishing Co., Inc.
866 Third Avenue, New York, N.Y. 10022
Collier-Macmillan Canada Ltd.

First Printing 1974
Printed in the United States of America

Library of Congress Cataloging in Publication Data

Eager, Fred.
The italic way to beautiful handwriting, cursive and calligraphic.

1. Writing, Italic. I. Title.
Z43.E118 1974b 652'.1 74-10506
ISBN 0-03-534580-X

Table of Contents

Getting Acquainted...

FOUR SCORE AND SEVEN YEARS AGO our fathers brought forth on this continent a new nation, conceived in Liberty, and dedicated to the proposition that all men are created equal. ¶ Now we are engaged in a great civil war, testing whether that nation, or any nation so conceived and so dedicated, can long endure. We are met on a great battlefield of that war. We have come to dedicate a portion of that field as a final resting place for those who here gave their lives that that nation might live. It is altogether fitting and proper that we should do this. ¶ But, in a larger sense, we cannot dedicate — we cannot consecrate — we cannot hallow this ground. The brave men, living and dead, who struggled here have consecrated it, far above our poor power to add or detract. The world will little note, nor long remember what we say here, but it can never forget what they did here. It is for us the living, rather, to be here dedicated here to the unfinished work which they who fought here have thus far so nobly advanced. It is rather for us to be here dedicated to the great task remaining before us — that from these honored dead we take increased devotion to that cause for which they gave the last full measure of devotion — that we here highly resolve that these dead shall not have died in vain — that this nation, under God, shall have a new birth of freedom — and that government of the people, by the people, for the people, shall not perish from the earth.

The Gettysburg Address — Abraham Lincoln

November 19, 1863

FOUR SCORE AND SEVEN YEARS AGO our fathers brought forth on this continent a new nation, conceived in Liberty, and dedicated to the proposition that all men are created equal. ¶ Now we are engaged in a great civil war, testing whether that nation, or any nation so conceived and so dedicated, can long endure. We are met on a great battlefield of that war. We have come to dedicate a portion of that field as a final resting place for those who gave their lives that that nation might live. It is altogether fitting and proper that we should do this. ¶ But, in a larger sense, we cannot dedicate – we can not consecrate – we cannot hallow – this ground. The brave men, living and dead, who struggled here have consecrated it, far above our poor power to add or detract. The world will little note, nor long remember what we say here, but it can never forget what they did here. It is for us the living, rather, to be dedicated here to the unfinished work which they who fought here have thus far so nobly advanced. It is rather for us to be here dedicated to the great task remaining before us – that from these honored dead we take increased devotion to that cause for which they gave the last full measure of devotion – that we here highly resolve that these dead shall not have died in vain – that this nation, under God, shall have a new birth of freedom – and that government of the people, by the people, for the people, shall not perish from the earth

The Gettysburg Address — Abraham Lincoln

November 19, 1863

FOUR SCORE AND SEVEN YEARS AGO our fathers brought forth on this continent a new nation, conceived in Liberty, and dedicated to the proposition that all men are created equal. ¶ Now we are engaged in a great civil war, testing whether that nation, or any nation so conceived and so dedicated, can long endure. We are met on a great battlefield of that war. We have come to dedicate a portion of that field as a final resting place for those who here gave their lives that that nation might live. It is altogether fitting and proper that we should do this. ¶ But, in a larger sense, we cannot dedicate – we cannot consecrate – we cannot hallow this ground. The brave men, living and dead, who struggled here have consecrated it far above our poor power to add or detract. The world will little note, nor long remember what we say here, but it can never forget what they did here. It is for us the living, rather, to be dedicated here to the unfinished work which they who fought here have thus far so nobly advanced. It is rather for us to be dedicated to the great task remaining before us – that from these honored dead we take increased devotion to that cause for which they gave the last full measure of devotion – that we here highly resolve that these dead shall not have died in vain – that this nation, under God, shall have a new birth of freedom – and that government of the people, by the people, for the people, shall not perish from the earth.

The Gettysburg Address Abraham Lincoln

November 19, 1863

Foreword

HE previous edition of 'Guide to Italic Handwriting' has been a most useful teaching aid which I have re-mmended to many of my students since I settled perm-nently in the U.S.A. two years ago.

lid not seek to replace Alfred Fairbank's 'A Handwriting lanual' (the earliest and still the classic 20th century anual), but it has added a very practical dimension the study of Italic by breaking it down into very detail-l steps, with emphasis laid on tracing and then copying e models in the manual itself. Fred Eager's books are great service to students in spreading sound teaching of e Italic style of writing throughout America and, I hope, ill be as useful abroad.

articularly welcome this completely up-dated edition of e 'Guide' because it is in tune with my own lines of think-g in recent years in facing the contradiction posed in ccessfully joining a compressed alphabet for fast writing. any teachers, including myself, have attempted to over-me this contradiction by teaching an average-width style, th a 45° pen angle, affording a compromise between the ight of each downstroke and sufficient thinness of diag-al joins. The following diagrams will better illustrate e mathematical problems involved when joins are used in a narrow Chancery style.

30° pen angle produces strong downstrokes and thinner horizontals (an ideal, natural proportion), but diagonal joins are thick and too obtrusive.

45° pen angle produces strong downstrokes but also heavy horizontals of equal thickness. Diagonal joins have some thickness.

60° pen angle produces thin, weak downstrokes and very thick, ugly horizontals. Yet diagonal joins are thin and unobtrusive.

vonder a 45° angle with an average width of letter s always been the compromise solution. Incident-ly, much can be learned from going further with experiments like the above, trying various combin-ations of pen-angle, width between strokes, letter height and writing slant using two pencils joined together or a two-pronged pen nib so that the structure may be seen clearly, then with a very broad, edged nib.

A strong downstr with a thick joi

Here we are shown a new solution based, not on compromise, but on a fresh look at 16th century models & the awareness of two major approaches. The condensed Italic used in countless formal mss. and documents, which have been the inspiration of the mod-ern revival, were treated formally and joined only rarely. Hands which employed many joins were more frequently based on much wider letter forms, and sometimes an increased forward slant. One of the most well-known of these examples, from the P. Victoris manuscript, owned by the late James Wardrop, beloved by him and by Alfred Fairbank, and now in the V. & A. Museum, London, greatly impressed me as a student. It is reproduced in Fairbank's manual, plate 4. The writing is so rhythmic and employs more joining of letters than any of the other early hands he reproduces, most of which show very little joining.

A strong downstr with a thin join

Mr Eager recognises that Italic can be taught in two distinct ways. He advocates the elegant, condensed form for more formal use, and a very open style with wide letters and equally wide spacing, where thin joins are easily achieved, for a fast, everyday cursive script which is legible & beautiful. It can hardly be coincidence that the 'free' italic (as distinct from the formal 'set' Italic) of so many professional calligraphers is open and flowing rather than narrow and spiky.

I have not seen a manual which approaches the problem by demonstrating this distinction and I commend the thought-ful research which has led to Mr Eager's solution and his easi-ly understood and comprehensive manual, which, if followed carefully, without merely dipping and skipping, should enable a student to master the Italic hand in its many facets in a surprisingly short while.

Sheila Waters ARCA

A formal model develops into a fast cursive for everyda use

ligraphed by Sheila Waters, Craft Member of the Society of Scribes and Illuminators, Bethesda, Maryland, December 1973

A Note to Teachers

For adequate progress with a class the following must be assumed:

1. The class will meet regularly.
2. The students will have time to do assignments between classes.
3. The students really teach or train themselves. They must build the habits in their hands. The teacher's primary role is to help this process along. Nothing is so devastating as wrong practice, therefore one of the most important functions of the teacher is to help the student see things he seems to be missing, encouraging, cajoling, correcting, admonishing, inspiring, and recommending necessary drill.

The class sessions will be primarily devoted to individual attention to work done between classes by the students, to presentation of historic and contemporary examples of calligraphy to inspire the work of the students, and to dictation for controlled speed practice.

Dictation can be used to build speed by starting slowly and gradually increasing speed in 1) repetition of one letter: a a a a, etc.; 2) repetition of one word; 3) repetition of a short phrase or saying; and 4) reading a story. You can pace the speed of dictation either by writing in the air yourself, by watching your students, or by using a pocket metronome, available at music stores. The metronome can be set at any speed from 40 letters per minute on up, and slower by counting two ticks per letter. Read aloud a word or group of words, then spell the words to yourself, one tick for each letter—two for capitals. Very short stories or amusing news items are useful for this dictation.

Purpose

The purpose of this book is to enable a student to develop two basic hands—one for special occasions and one for rapid handwriting, both beautiful and functional; to lay a foundation for calligraphic studies in the beautiful historic alphabets; and to awaken an interest in size, proportion, balance, tone, texture, which could carry one directly into wider experiences in the field of art.

Alert adults may teach themselves by thorough attention to all the instructions in the book, and faithful practice of the assignments. For the best certain progress of a student, a teacher is a great help, for encouragement, guidance, his examples, and especially his immediate criticism which helps a student avoid developing a bad habit which may later take much careful work to overcome.

?

Why write a completely new Guide to Italic Handwriting when the original of 1959 and its 1967 rewritten and expanded counterpart which added the trace-and-copy method have sold over twenty-six thousand copies and are still in popular demand?

The experience of the author with his students and a deeper study of spacing in many renaissance and modern Italic hands, have convinced him that there is a better way of teaching Italic both to satisfy the demands of the eye for beauty, the hand for rhythm and ease, the demands of today for speed, and again the demand of the eye for readability.

The demands of the eye for beauty and for readability are not the same, and the compromises forced on handwriting by the necessity of speed require a more varied approach in the method presented in handwriting instruction. In a word, writing for beauty and writing for speed should be correlated and developed at the same time. A practical development of both should be presented throughout the course, followed by examples of some of the possible compromises which each writer will be making on his own, as determined by taste and necessity.

Parallels to this dual approach in handwriting can be found in other arts:

READING: Speed: Try Evelyn Woods' Reading Dynamics courses presented throughout the nation. Slow: For reading out loud see Nedra N. Lamar's How to Speak the Written Word.

ART: Speed: The sketching of ideas to record impressions quickly. Slow: finished work for exhibit, decoration, individual expression, or for practical use such as in advertising.

PHOTOGRAPHY: Speed: Catching events when they happen. Slow: Portraiture, and other carefully planned works considering skillful placement of light, subject, and angles of shots.

MUSIC: Speed: Sight-reading to get the general impression of a composition. Slow: Detailed practice for performance or for pleasure.

Acknowledgments

Any man and his work are the fruit of his associations with many teachers, friends, acquaintances, students, exhibits, books, and in the case of this writer, correspondents. Each has contributed significantly to the final product, and if the reader approves the result, the credit really belongs to all of those whose generosity and courage to ellucidate, criticize, and encourage have resulted in something found to be of value to others. Then their labors and gifts can return some satisfaction. So many have contributed generously to the work of the author that the full list of acknowledgements to each reads as an autobiographic account. As such it has little merit in a textbook, and interested readers will find the account elsewhere.

But acknowledgements are due here

To Professor Lloyd J. Reynolds, whose encouragement and kind and generous criticism steered me in the right direction at the beginning of my Italic studies, and whose summer course at Reed College set a standard for me of detailed, thoughtful study of the alphabet. Always, as I write, I am grateful for the sure foundation which he helped me to build and for his pointing out the need to be especially careful when teaching others.

To James T. Mangan for permission to use "Write a Letter."

To Miss Juanita J. Miller for permission to reprint three verses from Joaquin Miller's poem, "Columbus."

To Carl W. Meyer for his original euphonious nonsense words.

To The Christian Science Monitor for permission to reprint Emilie Glenn's "Eyecrobatics," © 1960 and Milton Kaplan's "The Swans," © 1973 by The Christian Science Publishing Society. All rights reserved.

To George Miller for "Notes on Pen Grinding."

To Faber and Faber, Ltd. for permission to quote from "A Handwriting Manual" by Alfred Fairbank.

To all whose handwriting is reproduced on pages 13, 14, and 96 to 100.

Special acknowledgment is deserved by Mrs. Sheila Waters, professional calligrapher, who is known to Italic buffs by her design on the cover of the Society for Italic Handwriting Journal. Deep appreciation is due her for her one lesson that opened my eyes to entirely new paths of discovery and led directly to the rewriting of all my books; for her continuing interest and unstinting helpful criticism, which has been a great encouragement in the carrying out of this task.

And to Joanne, my beloved wife for her patience during the studies for and writing of the text, and for the final editing of this edition.

The Two Primary Modes of Italic Handwriting

Calligraphic

This is a mode of writing based on the Renaissance "Chancery Cursive" models in the handwriting copy books of Arrighi, Palatino, Tagliente, Mercator, Lucas, and the formal manuscripts written by these scribes. Distinctive features of this hand are the x-height of the letters which is between four and five pen-widths, the even spacing of vertical strokes and the consistent angle of the pen when diagonal joins are not used. When diagonal joins are used, either they are at a steeper pen angle than that used for the letters themselves, or the spacing pattern is changed and more space occurs between the joined letters. This is the formal Italic that is practiced in the work of today's calligraphers: Alfred Fairbank, Raymond F. Da Boll, Paul Standard, Arnold Bank, Sheila Waters, Irene Wellington, Heather Child, and others.

In this writing, the spacing is set by the choice of width determined by the artist for his o's and u's. This may vary from work to work, but the choice of width for spacing is usually rather narrow. This writing is necessarily slower, more consistent and more beautiful. It has primary appeal to the eye. The ease of reading it, with our modern eyes accustomed to roman type, depends on the width of the spacing and the quality of the arches at the tops of the letters. If the width is greater, and the arches more curved or elliptical, easy reading is assured. If the spacing is narrower and the arches spikey, the reading is inhibited.

If only this mode of writing is learned, the student necessarily has several choices or tendencies. 1. To always write slowly. 2. To spoil the spacing by adding joins for speed. 3. To have a hand for top speed which tends to become spikey and difficult to read.

This mode, which we call calligraphic, looks formal because it is not joined, and the spacing is rather narrow, but a student who masters this hand and wishes to develop skill and versatility in the many historic calligraphic alphabets, will learn the Formal Set Italic in which all the strokes are pulled. For example, the letter a, taught in this book as one stroke, is made in three strokes: *a*

Cursive

This mode of writing is based on the Renaissance manuscripts recommended by Edward Johnston in Writing and Illuminating and Lettering for a cursive handwriting (see pages 280-287); on the plates included by Alfred Fairbank in both A Handwriting Manual and A Book of Scripts; and the writing in modern days by Edward Johnston, James Wardrop, Alfred Fairbank, Paul Standard, and others, but to this date, NOT taught in any handwriting books or manuals in print.

Distinguishing features of this hand are an x-height which is three to three and one-half pen widths, a rather wide spacing which is set by the rhythm of the hand as it joins letters together, and a consistent angle of the pen while using joins throughout.

In this mode of writing the spacing is set by the angle of the pen used in joins. The upper arches of the letters are generally curved and there must be a horizontal thrust which causes a more predominantly horizontal movement of the pen. The author feels that in this hand more readability with more speed are possible, for the edged pen exerts greater control at this smaller scale of writing. The rounded arches and greater width of spacing within and between the letters tends to make the distinctive shapes of the letters clearer to the eye.

The primary objection to this hand seems to be that, at any speed, it does not have the beauty of the texture of the Calligraphic mode with its close spacing, but it more than makes up for this shortcoming by simplicity, practicality, speed and readability.

The work in this book alternates between the Calligraphic mode and the Cursive mode so that you can develop rhythm at the same time as you are developing ideal letter shapes.

How to Use This Book

IMPORTANT:

Rapid progress is insured if a student will:

1. Read ALL INSTRUCTIONS and follow them implicitly.

2. When new material is presented, TRACE the model by writing directly on it, then COPY the model carefully in the space adjacent to, or directly below, it. The problems of ANY STUDENT WHO DOES NOT make progress can be directly traced to his reluctance to follow instructions or to write ON the models in the book.

3. Some students will learn new material more quickly than others. If your copying looks EXACTLY like the model, then in further practice on the same material, you should copy the models on your own paper, using a guide sheet from the back of the book. Save the models and spaces in the book for later review if desired. The author has marked an * at places where a student may start to copy the models on his own paper. "NEW" indicates new material which should be TRACED and COPIED. On the work pages, T means TRACE and C means COPY.

4. Before you start, collect about five pages of your present handwriting, and put the date on them. As you progress, place two pages of your work on a bulletin board—one calligraphic, one cursive. ALWAYS date your papers. When you improve, replace the exhibits with your improvements. Keep all of your papers in a folder and the visible progress will encourage you. BEFORE and AFTER examples of students are a great encouragement for those who haven't studied Italic and think it is difficult.

5. If you are teaching yourself, be critical enough to see what you need to improve, but not so critical that you become discouraged. Praise yourself for your progress, as measured by viewing how far you have come, and encourage yourself to further progress, but don't become so elated that you lose the self-critical faculty. If you find no faults at all, you will cease to improve. If you see something that needs improvement and work at it, you will make steady progress.

6. Try to find a friend, who is also learning Italic, with whom you can visit or correspond. Always it is easier to see someone else's faults than your own, even from the beginning, and you both can be a great help in encouraging and criticizing each other.

7. Another help would be for you to teach Italic to someone who is interested as soon as you are far enough along to see your own errors and to correct them.

8. CONSTANTLY REVIEW. This will help fill the void caused by having no teacher to remind you that you have forgotten something!

9. Write notes to people or reminders to yourself, even the first week. Why learn to write beautifully if you never write? Write as much as you can, but slowly at first.

10. BEWARE. Do not try consciously to develop your own style. It will develop naturally as you make the decisions described in the last section of this book and as you gain sureness, freedom and speed. Throughout the first part of the book try to make your copy look EXACTLY like the model.

11. PACING. A student should try to finish the first section on basic letter shapes and spacing in one week.

Materials Needed

Lessons	Materials
1 - 11	A nylon-tipped pen with a point the width of the models. Notebook paper (8-1/2 x 11) with line-spacing the same as in this book.
12 - 28	Fountain pen with Italic broad nib. White paper on which ink will not feather; your thin lines will not spread; and which is thin enough so that the guide lines may easily be seen when placed underneath. Paper clips.
29 - 43	Fountain pen with Italic medium nib. Paper and paper clips as above.
44	Fountain pen with Italic fine nib.

Italic Models and Free Handwriting

Italic possesses characteristics which tend to preserve legibility as the hand gains freedom and speed. At the same time, mastery of the ideal brings sufficient pleasure to the learner so that the results seem to him to warrant the effort necessarily involved.

Italic gives even the beginner some degree of satisfaction right from the start, encouraging him to go on.

Below are samples of writing of students before and after Italic study, including the writing of a 9th grader, a college student and three adults, including a senior citizen.

On page 96 you will find the handwriting of children in 2nd, 4th, 7th and 12th grades. It is interesting to see how much variety can develop, even when the same precise model is used with a number of students.

On pages 97 to 100 you will find examples of the handwriting of adults who have written Italic for varying periods of time.

You may judge this variety of hands for yourself to see how close they are to the ideal models we have set up. You may then decide how to form your own personal hand, and choose which faults are the most grave, needing special practice to overcome. Now apply this same criticism to your own hand, and you will find that your own writing will continue to improve month after month and year after year.

Your Present Handwriting

Let's take a look at your present handwriting, so that you have a basis of comparison as you learn Italic and develop freedom and speed.

Everyone writes at a different speed, according to his own individuality and habits. You should expect to write Italic at least as fast as your present handwriting.

Take this speed test so you will be able to determine when Italic reaches the practicality of your present handwriting. If you are used to writing slowly you won't expect Italic to double your speed, but you may increase your speed to some extent.

Using your customary writing tool, write your name and the date at the top of a piece of paper. Then write the following sentence: A quick brown fox jumps over the lazy dog. Draw a short line below this sentence to separate it from the timed portion which follows.

Now write this sentence at your normal handwriting speed, as many times as you can in two minutes. Count the number of complete sentences and multiply by 33. Add the letters you may have in the incomplete sentence and divide by two. This gives you your present writing speed in l.p.m. (letters per minute).

Keep this sheet for comparison when you start building speed with your Italic hand on page 75.

EXAMPLES OF WRITING BEFORE AND AFTER ITALIC STUDY

A College Student

Dear Mr. Eager:

Here is my ordinary handwriting before I switched to italic I think it is legible enough, but not nearly so nice to look at as an italic script. Being a student of Renaissance literature, I would much rather write with a hand the writers of that period used than with an ordinary cursive.

Gregory W. Payne
2230 Haste St. Apt. 202
Berkeley, California 94704

16 February 1969

Dear Mr. Eager:

I have been writing with an italic script now for about five months. Since I am a student at the University of California, I must use handwriting quite a bit. My "practice sessions" are my classes, since I now take notes in italic. My classmates have often embarassed me, in fact, by praising my handwriting too much!

My interest in italic began this summer, when I noticed a friend of mine from Oxford writing with what I thought an unusual pen. I enquired at a stationers (Campbell's, in Westwood, Ca.) and was shown your Guide to Italic Handwriting. This Christmas, I had to buy italic pens for my whole family, since they were all so interested.

It occurs to me that you could 'push' italic on our university campuses, since so many of my friends have shown an interest. My thanks to you, also, for recommending Artone ink, which is the best consistency I have found. I hope to continue perfecting my hand, since I haven't yet really mastered the letter-shapes.

Very truly yours,
Gregory W. Payne

A Senior Citizen

Dear Mr. Yager:

Enclosed is a sample of my Italic writing; not the best, but at 76 I am still trying to perfect same and receive great pleasure from the compliments of all my friends and relatives.

Italimuse, Inc.
Grand Island, N.Y.

October 24, 1968
54 May Drive
Chatham, N.J.

Dear Mr. Yager:

I acknowledge receipt of the Summary of Italic Handwriting and in reply, advise you that I attended the Madison-Chatham, N.J. Adult Night School in the fall of 1966. Class teacher, Mrs. Gretchen Wolpert of Short Hills, N.J. At this time I just passed my Seventy-fourth birthday, consequently I have been writing Italic two years. I write all my correspondence in Italic including my personel checks. I try to practive the alphabet twice a week, for fifteen minute peroids. All my relatives that I correspond with are amazed with my writing, all have advised me they show it to their friends. At this date I am addressing Fourty-two cards to be used at table settings at our local golf club. For Christmass 1967, I wrote my own Christmas Cards and propose the same action for 1968.

I purchased the Guide to Italic Handwriting when I attended classes in 1966.

Sincerely Yours,
Howard B. Berrian

My old hand looks like this; I'm not taking as much care writing this, but it's about as fast as italic. To be perfectly truthful my old hand has changed some too because of the change in the way I hold a pen. Many of the things in the 'guide' have become second nature now.

July 22, 1973
1908 Gail Court
Loveland, Colo. 80537

Dear Mr. Eager,

I purchased the Guide to Italic Handwriting from Italimuse in February 1973. I spend some time every day, sometimes an hour or more. Unfortunately the summer season has caused me to miss practice more than I like, but I have always practiced at least three times a week.

The new hand has been rewarding; it has attracted the attention of family and friends. I've started using italic in my work; its coming, but I want to be able to write faster without losing legibility. I can see the improvement as I pactice and I intend to keep at it.

Sincerely yours,

Will Cowan

Ninth Grade

Kim Williams
October 30, 1972

French
Homework

1) Il apprends le français. Il étudie -
Il apprends le francais en étudiant.
2) Je parle à mon père. Je mange.
Je parle à mon père en mangant.

whatsoever things are true, whatsoever things are honest, whatsoever things are just, whatsoever things are pure, whatsoever things are lovely, whatsoever things are of good report, if there be any virtue
if there be any praise,
think on these things
St. Paul to the Philippians

After 2-1/2 Weeks

Kim Williams

up until May, 1970, when I bought your guide to Italic Handwriting". — this was pretty much my typical handwriting —

25 May, 1970

Dear Mr. Eager;

We've been at this since 5/12. The capitals are faked, we've only finished lesson 12.

This is written with a broad nib dip pen, using home-made sepia ink (5 pts. red to 2 pts. green ink.) We are at a point where one becomes impatient with and critical of one's progress.

Very truly yours,
Charles J. Olender

8 Eden Avenue, Tonawanda, New York — 14150

July 31, 1970

Mr. Fred Eager,
c/o Italimuse,
Grand Island, New York.

Dear Fred;

This will indicate my progress to date. I've been at italics for almost three months; the first month I averaged 1/2 hour daily practice, often repeating a lesson 'til it "felt" right. Recently, my practice sessions have been much curtailed, often being no more than an occasional memo; and sometimes only a shopping list. I'm now starting daily alphabet practice, and progress should resume.

As inept as my hand is at present, I'm immensely pleased at the improvement over my former handwriting -- I've enclosed a sample.

Following your advice, I'm forcing my speed to improve fluency, and it's helping - this is my "fast" hand.

Many thanks to you for introducing me to italics.

Sincerely

Chuck Olender.

Let's Get Started . . .

Writing Position

POSITIONS FOR RIGHT-HANDED WRITERS

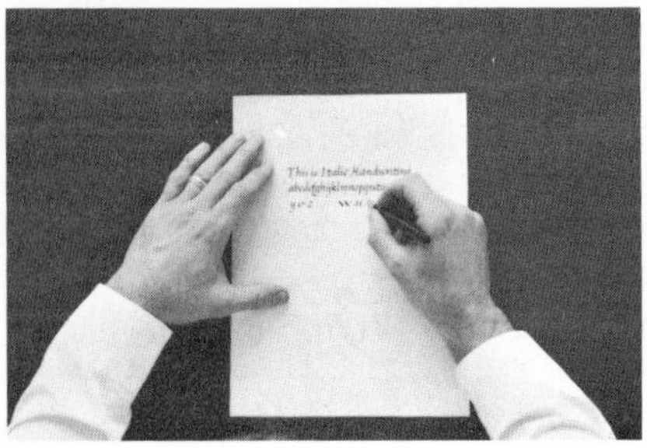

AT THE DESK

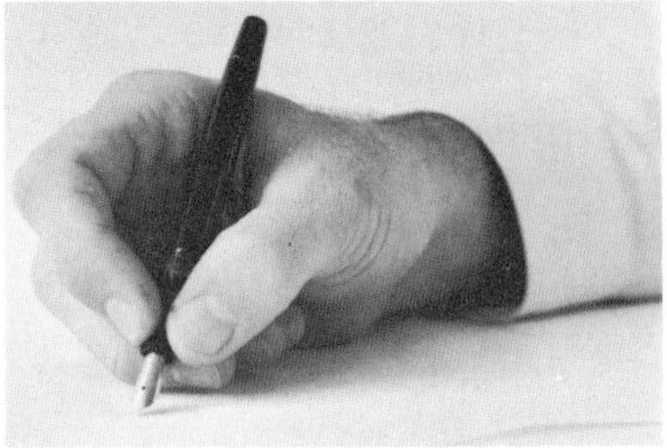

PEN - HOLD

The slant of the paper on the desk depends on the relation in the height of the desk to the height of the chair and on the writer's habits. It is preferable to have the paper as straight as possible.

POSITIONS FOR LEFT-HANDED WRITERS. Decide on one of these positions as soon as possible.

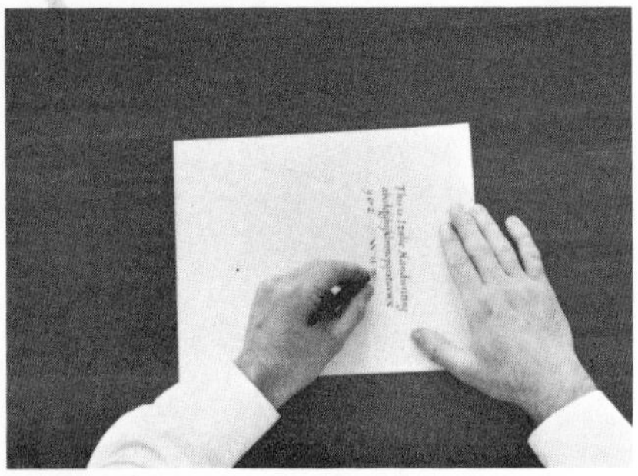

1.

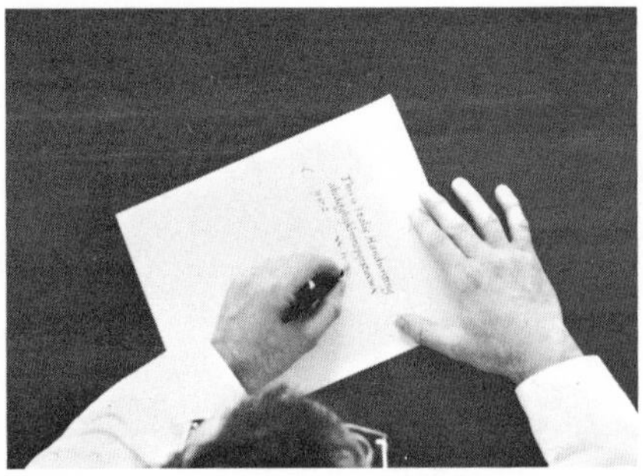

2.

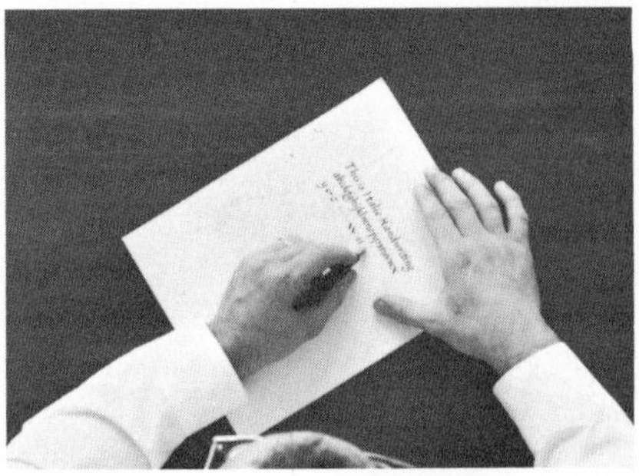

3.

The pen-hold for left-handed writers is the mirror image of that for the right-handed, but the hand may be turned flatter, depending on which writing position is used.

1. In the first position shown, the student may use the straight (square-cut) pens which right-handed writers use. These are available in all widths.
2. In the second position the student needs the 'left oblique' pens, available in Broad, Medium and Fine.
3. In the third position the 'left-hand' pens are needed. The nib has a straight edge on a 30° turn and is available in Medium and Fine widths only.

INCORRECT PEN-HOLDS: Common mistakes in holding the pen.

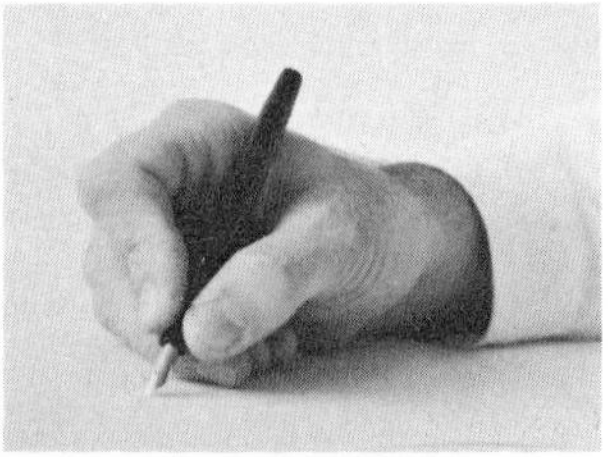

"Pushed finger"

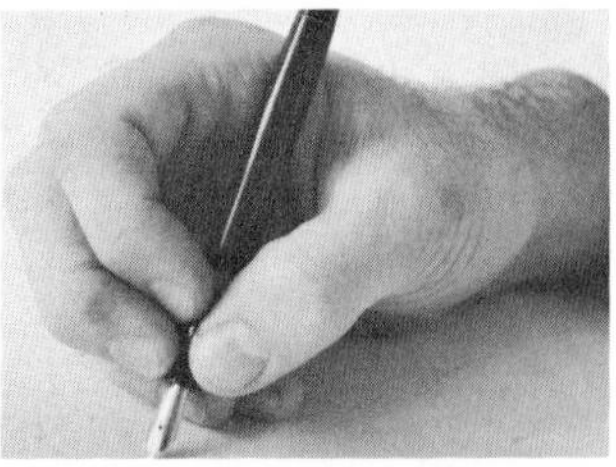

"Middle finger up"

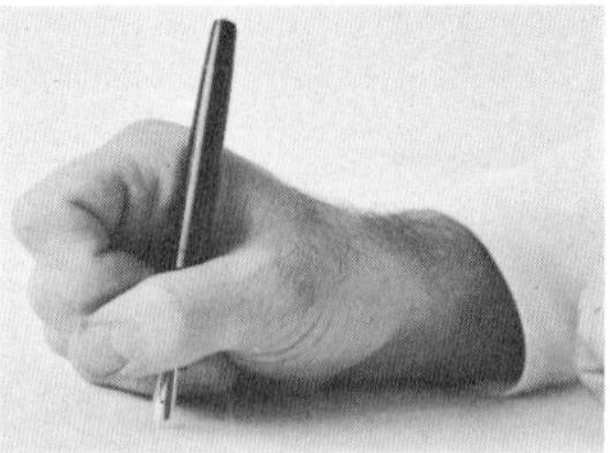

"Thumb advanced"

"Hooked hand"

NOTE: If your hand tightens or you feel tension in your hand and wrist as you are practicing, DON'T WORRY. It is a result of your concentrated effort to do well at something new. Give your hand frequent rests, shake it. In time you will learn to relax more AS you write.

Project I

The Calligraphic Mode of Italic Handwriting
Posture - Penhold - Basic Shapes - Spacing

The purpose of this project is to learn the basic Italic shapes and spacing, and to become accustomed to the correct posture and pen-hold.

Use a nylon-tip pen with a thickness like that of the models. While you are working on these pages, buy some notebook or yellow legal pad paper with lines spaced as on these pages, to use for review at the end of this section or for extra practice; or you may use plain white paper with Guide Sheet L on page 112.

First, study the pictures on page 16, and as you work, try to keep the correct posture and pen-hold.

The term TRACE & COPY as used in this book means to TRACE by writing directly on the model, then COPY the letter or word in the space provided. You are drawing the letters to learn the basic principles of letter formation.

LESSON 1: SIMPLE LETTERS WITH VERTICALS—SPACING

Become accustomed to even spacing by means of the simpler letters of the alphabet. As you draw each line be conscious of the spaces already made and make new spaces which conform to the old. DO NOT look only at what you are writing. Look at the spaces you are making between your lines.

TRACE by writing directly on the model. Discover the pattern set up at the beginning of the line and copy it for the entire line, working from the model into the blank space at the end of the line when you are on your own. Make your copy look exactly like the model.

ALWAYS begin at the dot and follow the direction of the arrows.

TRACE COPY

Do not lift pen for u

Do not lift pen for n

ALWAYS use very light pressure

Trace and Copy

NOTICE how the letters OVERLAP the guide lines. Do not miss the guide lines!: iii

CONTINUE the groups of letters to the end of the line

Trace and Copy

Serifs provide graceful entrances and exits for many letters: *i i u u*

Sharp serif

T&C

Curved serif

Trace and Copy

At first, draw the letters very slowly to establish the feeling and thinking of the ideal shapes and their spacing.

T&C

This finishing stroke for the j should be a flat, horizontal push stroke

T&C nmh nmh nmh

TRACE to the arrow, then COPY below

Same as u

TRACE ijhlmnruyijhlmnruyijhn

Same as for j

COPY→

LESSON 2: THE ELLIPSE: o, and e

Notice in spacing the elliptical letters, that the curve of the ellipse is actually placed closer to a straight line (as in i, h, l, u) than another straight line would be. But the optical appearance is even spacing. Similarly, a curved line is placed even closer to another curved line for even-appearing optical spacing. See the rules for spacing on page 29.

T&C llollolloll llollo

In o your elliptical stroke pushes around the top and back to the starting point

Notice that e and o start with DOWN strokes which curve flatly to the left.

T&C llceeelle lle lle lle

e is made in two strokes. The second stroke pulls around and tucks horizontally into the middle.

T&C llmoonllmoonll ll

Trace a word, copy it below, then next word

TRACE omen, hole, money, lonely,

COPY:

T&C him her him her

How is your posture? Are you sitting up?

Notice that the beginning serif of t starts just below the waist line, goes just above the waist line, then sharply down. The cross stroke starts where the serif begins

Waist line

1 2

T&C t + ‾ = t iit tiit tiit ... tiit

You can easily join the cross-stroke of t or f to the next down stroke

TRACE ııtome, ıı linen, ıı rim, ıı jury, ıı

COPY →

Notice that f does not reach up all the way to the ascender line.
Notice that very little of the cross stroke of f is on the left side of the vertical.
For double ff's, draw the two down-strokes first, then cross both with one stroke.
Don't let double ff's crowd together closer than other vertical lines.

scender line

T&C ijfl ijfl ... muffle

Base line

Descender line

TRACE efhijlmnortu, efhijlmnort,

COPY →

T ornery, front, horticulture,

C →

Hereafter instructions to trace a line will be shown by T and to copy a line by C or by an arrow.

him

STOP for Some Theory & Principles

LESSON 3: RELATIONSHIPS OF THE LETTERS TO EACH OTHER

PLEASE pay very careful attention to the following descriptions. Go over them again and again, tracing the models lightly with a PENCIL until you are certain that you fully understand them and can make the movements involved. This understanding is most important if you are to have acceptable results with the Calligraphic Mode of Italic.

All of the letters of the alphabet can be related to the oblong parallelogram, and are shown here in their various groups, built on parallelograms.

NOTICE how the curves of o, e, c, a, d, g, q, b, and p overlap the vertical sides of the parallelogram.

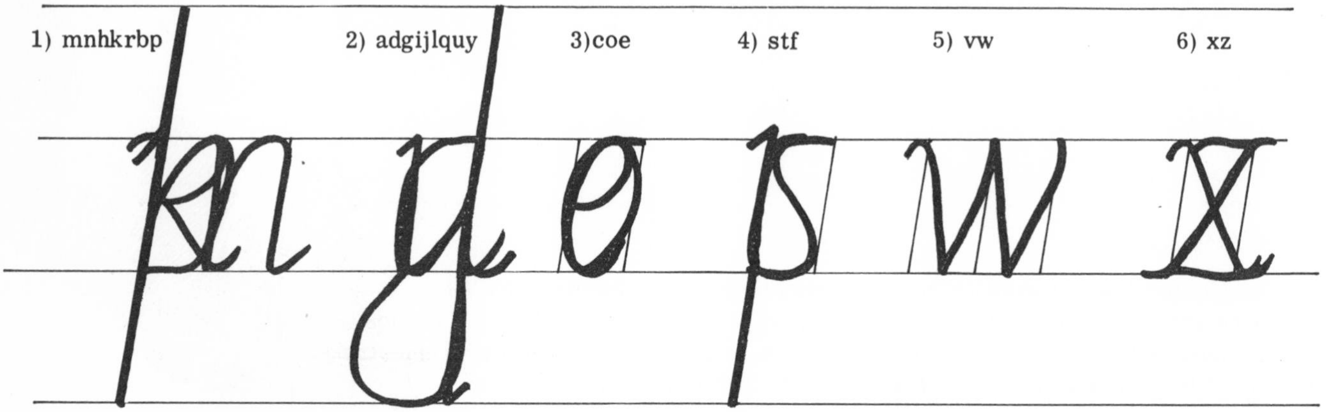

All of the letters of the alphabet can also be related to the ellipse; but, when branching is involved, the letter line cuts away from the ellipse for a moment. Here letters are shown in their various groups, built on ellipses.

NOTICE that it is in the narrow curves of a, d, g, q, u, y, m, n, h, k, r, b, p that the letters cut away from the ellipse.

NOTICE that the branching happens at about the middle of the x-height of the letter in all of the letters just mentioned. At that point the line branches gently away from the main vertical stem of the letter.

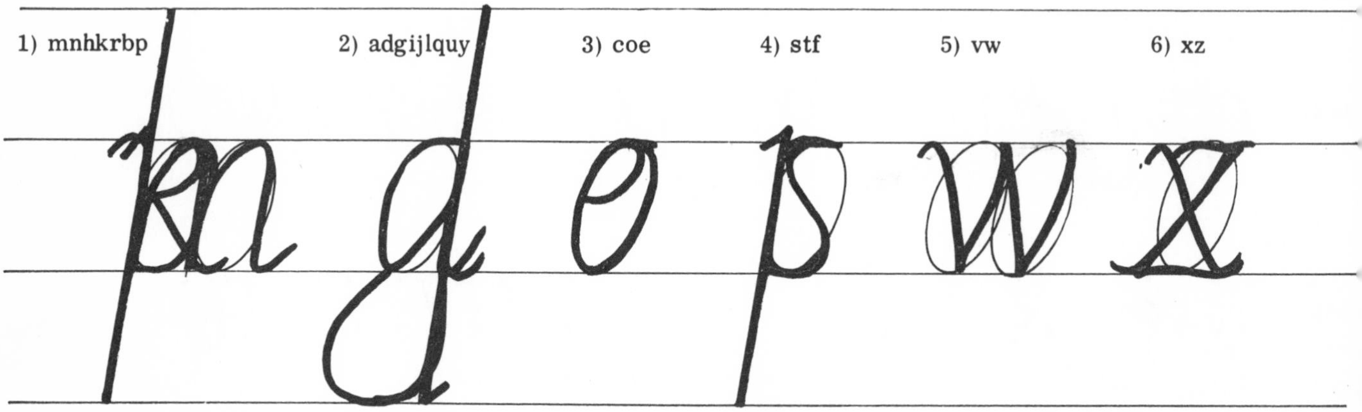

On the parallelograms and ellipses below write the letters you have learned on pages 18 and 19:

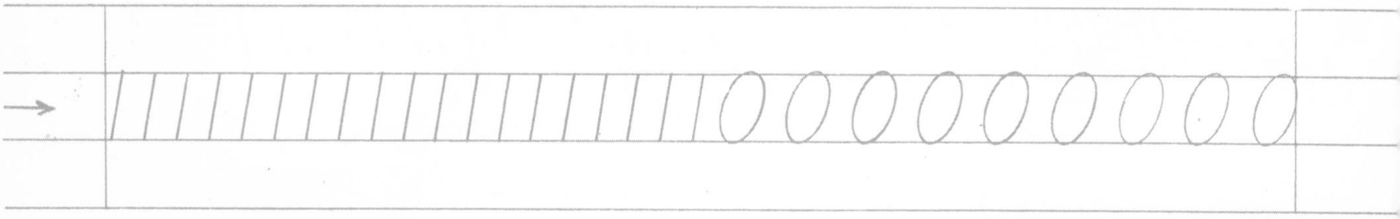

In the following lessons you will be building letters on parallelograms, ellipses, or in blank spaces.

You may have additional optional practice by using white paper with Guide Sheet L on page 112. Use the portion of the Guide Sheet which has the slanted vertical guide lines.

ESSON 4: m, n, h, k, r.

PLEASE NOTICE CAREFULLY the important points about each letter group: m, n, h, k, r, b, and p all have the principle of "branching." The first stroke goes down to the base-line, then springs up, retracing the same path to a point HALF-WAY up to the waist line, where it branches gently out, but cutting across the ellipse, it meets the right side of the ellipse at the top and follows it into a vertical down-stroke parallel to the first down-stroke.

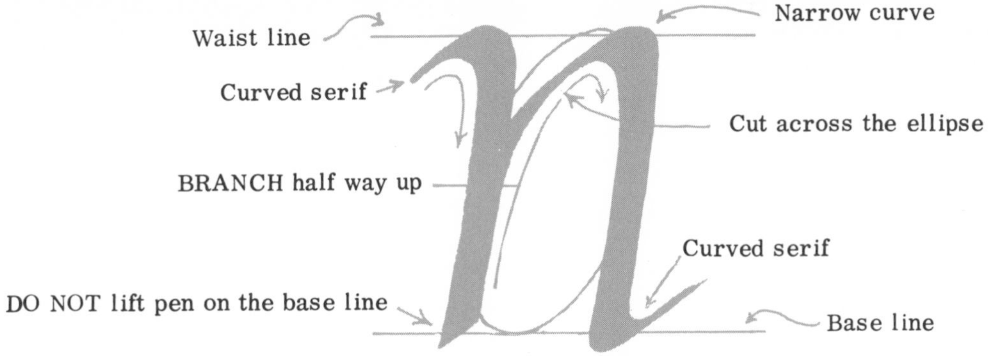

Build these letters on ellipses and parallelograms. Begin at the dots.— NOT

T & C

For letter m remember the same points as for n, but branch twice. NOT

T&C

Remember to cut across the ellipse for a narrower curve. NOT

T&C

Should be straight. NOT r branches high and ends with a short horizontal stroke NOT

T&C

Write directly on one word, then COPY it below. Then the next word.

T

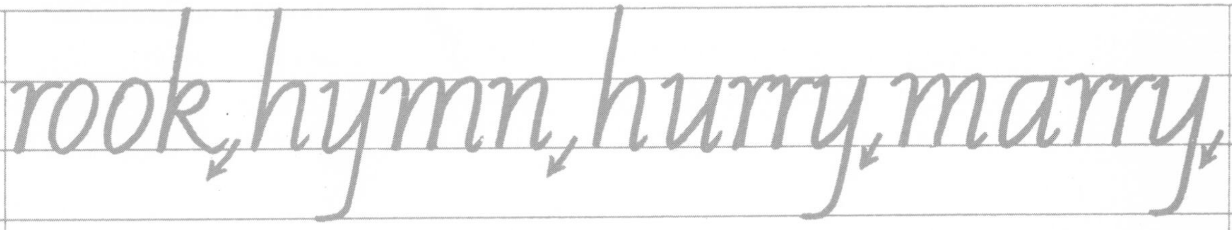

C →

Check slant & spacing by drawing light lines through verticals (use a ruler)

LESSON 5: b and p. These letters contain the a-shape inverted and reversed (ɒ).

For b follow carefully these points:

1. Straight down from the ascender line.
2. Retrace up WITHOUT LIFTING pen to a point half-way up to the waist line.
3. Branch up to the waist line on the right side of the ellipse (cutting across the ellipse)
4. Make a narrow curve
5. Follow the ellipse, making the right side as parallel to the left side as is possible with a curved line.
6. Shoulder in rather squarely with a push flat along the bottom.

DO NOT LIFT YOUR PEN WHILE WRITING b

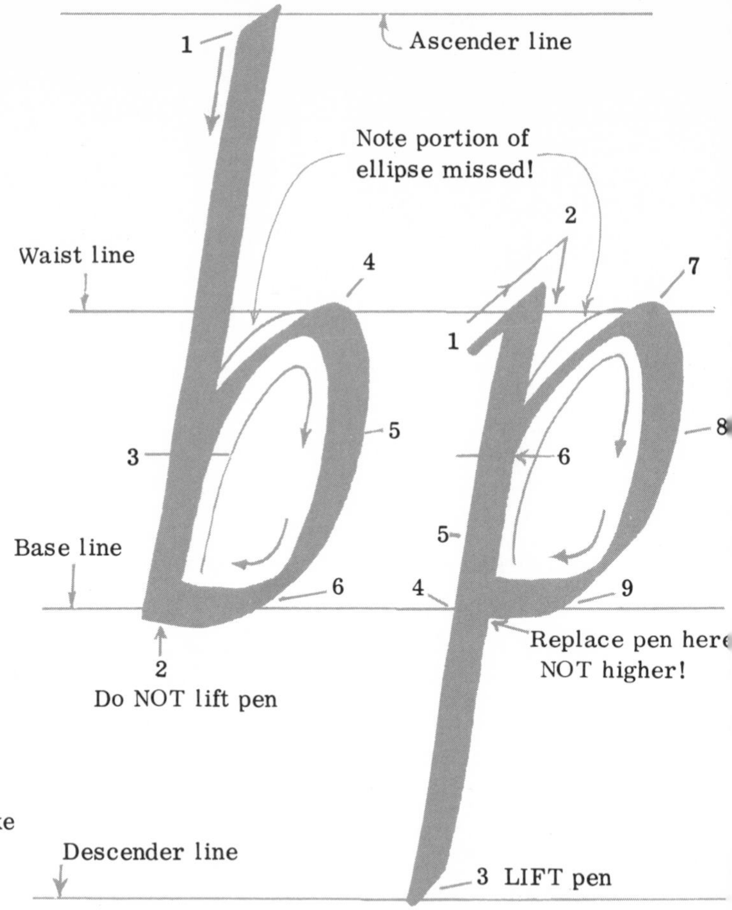

For p follow carefully these points:

1. Serif starts just below and moves to just above the waist-line
2. Sharply down to the descender line
3. LIFT PEN
4. Replace pen on the BASE-LINE, NOT above it
5. Retrace up to a point half way to the waist-line
6. Branch up to the waist-line on the right side of the ellipse
7. Make a narrow curve
8. Follow the ellipse parallel to the first down-stroke
9. Shoulder in rather squarely with a push flat along the bottom.

To get the feeling of the narrow curve and the shoulder in b and p shapes, you MUST slow down. It often helps to write the letters at first with angular corners, actually stopping the pen at the corners. Try to remember the feel of n and h, but push in at the bottom.

Build b's and p's on ellipses and parallelograms

When this is easy, go over the same letters again, but this time without stopping, just slowing down at the corners. Perfect b's and p's will result. Be sure to always go up the main stem and branch up to the narrow curve.

NOT 

NOT 

T&C hhbbppbpbp bp

T bubble, bonnet, bumper,

C →

T puppy, moppet, umpire,

C →

LESSON 6: s, f, and t

These letters are related because of their horizontal strokes. t begins like p with a serif that goes just above the waist-line. The top of the cross stroke must be just under the line and touching it. t is a SMALL letter without an ascender. NOT t t t t t c

T&C tttt t ff ff f

f isn't as tall as l, h, k. It starts with a push-stroke and has a cross-stroke like t. NOT fff

s begins and ends with a flat push-stroke and fits into an ellipse. The middle of s should be diagonal (\ ): The upper curve should appear the same size as the lower curve. Turn the page upside down and you will see that it is actually smaller. NOT s s s s s s

T&C ssss ss s s

T&C soft fist bust

LESSON 7: c, o, e, l, t.

Notice that these letters have an elliptical lower curve while a, d, g, q, u, and y have narrow lower curves. (For closer spacing these curves may sometimes have to be narrower.)

Both o and e begin with a DOWN stroke: o e not o e

ALWAYS write e in two strokes. It will keep the eye of e open so that when writing rapidly it will never be confused with i's. Later you will learn the nice e joins: eeeeee

NOT e e e e e e

oo e e eoeoe oe oe oe

c begins with a flat push-stroke, then follows the ellipse. NOT c c c c

ccc cc cc cc cc cc

coetl coetl

T cloth, comet, collection, lot,

C →

T orioles, cocoon, echo, people,

C →

buffoon tilt

LESSON 8: a-shapes (a, d, g, q); u and y

This shape has the same inside counter (white space) as the b's and p's, inverted and reversed. Your shapes will match in these two families if you pay special attention to these points:

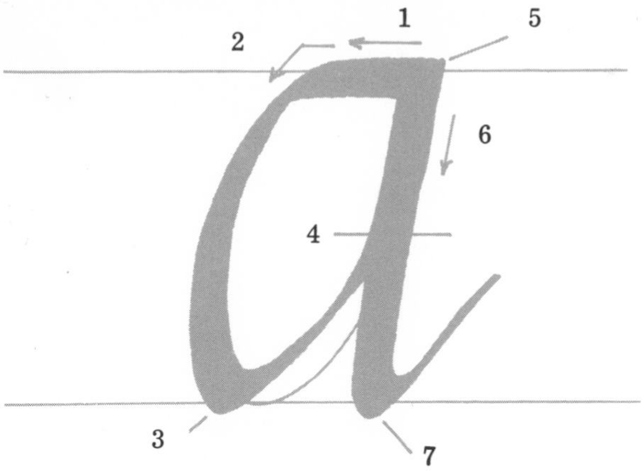

1. Push flat across the top
2. Shoulder down rather squarely and follow the ellipse to the base line on the left side of the ellipse. (Aim OUT and to the LEFT on this downstroke.
3. Make a narrow turn and cut across the ellipse to
4. A point half-way up to the waist line,
5. Then straight up to the starting point.
   ALL OF THE a-shapes start with this one-stroke pocket shape:  . For EACH letter the pen should return to the starting point. Only the letter d has a pen lift which is at this starting point. For letters a, g, and q, the pen should stay on the paper for one continuous stroke.
6. Straight down to the base line. This causes the strokes to look like inverted branching at No. 4.
7. End with a narrow curve matching the curve at No. 3, lifting the pen in a light up-stroke which parallels the stroke from 3 to 4.

DO NOT LIFT YOUR PEN while writing a

NOT 

To get the feeling of the shoulder and narrow curve in a-shapes, you MUST slow down. It often helps to write the letter at first with angular corners, actually stopping the pen at the corners.

When this is comfortable, go over the same letters again, but this time NOT stopping, just slowing down at the corners. Perfect a's will result.
Another help is, after making the top, think "u."

For g, points 1 - 5 are identical with those for the a-shape. REVIEW THEM.

6. Straight down to the descender line with a slight arch (not too much)
7. Then a happy, free, open curve back to the narrow curve (No. 3) and LIFT the pen. DO NOT LIFT the pen when writing g, until you reach No. 3.

NOT 

For q, points 1-5 are identical with those for the a-shape.
6. Straight down with NO arch to the baseline,
7. Light sharp up-stroke serif, lifting the pen.
DO NOT LIFT YOUR PEN while writing q.

q NOT

qq qq q q qq qq q

For d, points 1-4 are identical to the other a-shapes, BUT
5. At 5, the starting point, LIFT your pen, DO NOT LIFT your pen BEFORE you reach this point (No. 5).
6. Now place the pen on the ascender line at 6 and straight down to the baseline, retracing the line from 5 - 4 on the way, and
7. End with a narrow curve matching the curve at 3, and lifting the pen in a light up-stroke which parallels the stroke from 3 - 4.

6

d = d NOT

DO NOT lift the pen here, or the d looks shapeless

dd d dd d drag

For u, begin with a light up-stroke serif, then straight down. Now follow points 3 - 7 for drawing a NOT

uu uu quaint

y begins like u and ends like j NOT

yy yy y yucca

equip remedy

T gauge, rag, aqueduct, dad,

C →

LESSON 9: v, w, x, z

Both v and w start with a curving serif which goes steeply down to an angle, overlaps the base-line, then rising, turns in (to avoid confusion with r). The slant of these letters is determined by a line drawn from the angle to a point midway in the opening above. vw

vv ww

NOT v v v v v v

vwvw vw vw

xx

The first stroke of x has curved serifs at the beginning and end. The second stroke has a flat beginning and end.

NOT x x x x x

The top and bottom of z curve just a little. The diagonal is straight. The bottom is wider than the top. The down-stroke should go past the beginning of the letter to establish the forward slope

zz

NOT z z z z z

xzxz xz xz xz

T wave, zany, ox, youth, axe,

C →

T vivid wax buzz azure sax

C →

varsity syrinx

LESSON 10: REVIEW DO NOT WRITE on this page. Save it for review and reference.

1. REVIEW OF NUMBER OF STROKES

These letters are made in one continous stroke of the pen WITHOUT lifting the pen from the paper:

One-stroke abcghijklmnoqrsuvwyz

These letters are made in two strokes, and you MUST LIFT the pen to make the second stroke:

Two-stroke dd ee f pp tt x

2. REVIEW OF ENTRANCES AND EXITS

The following letters start with a sharp-angled serif; as do v, w, x when they are preceded by a join:

Sharp entrances ijptuy (vwx)

The following letters start with a curved serif; as do v, w, x when they are NOT preceded by a join:

Curved entrances mnrvwx

The following letters end with a narrow lower curve:

Narrow Lower curve adhimnu humming

The following letters end with a fuller, elliptical lower curve:

But these curves may sometimes have to be narrower for closer spacing.

Elliptical Lower curve celot Lancelot

3. IMPORTANT: Review by writing the entire alphabet on your own paper, each letter three times: aaa, bbb, ccc, ddd, etc. Underline the one which you feel is the best. To mark off your paper, use notebook paper with spaces the same as those we have been using in this section. Skip the first line and mark off every third space as you see we have done on the preceding pages. These spaces are for the x-height of each letter. When you are finished, check your work with the model and notice especially adgq, bp, mn, s.

If you don't remember the principles for the letter you are writing and want to look at it again the first time it was presented you can locate it quickly by referring to the Table of Contents. Be sure to read the instructions by the model, because if you have forgotten the shape, you probably have forgotten the principles for that letter, too.

Don't be discouraged if you need to look back, it is quite usual for students to need this review at this point in their work.

Alphabet Review aaabbbcccdddeeefff etc.

LESSON 11: THEORY AND PRACTICE OF SPACING IN THE CALLIGRAPHIC MODE

IMPORTANT: Carefully study these rules for spacing and the examples given. TRACE and COPY these pages on spacing, then take words from the list which follows, one at a time. Alternating between the vertical guide line portion and the lower portion of Guide Sheet "L", write each word three times, improving the spacing each time. Continue practicing spacing in this way on a regular basis while you progress into the following lessons. More than anything else, consistent slant and even spacing give a page of writing a patterned beauty that makes it the envy of those who have neglected this important study.

You will be able to look at your spacing more objectively if you turn your paper upside down. When it is right-side up, you see your old friends, the alphabet and recognizable words, and are distracted from looking at the spacing. Upside down, the shapes are not familiar—the appearance is more like that of an abstract design, so you can be more conscious of spacing patterns. You will notice lighter color where you have left too much space and dark patches where you have crowded your vertical strokes.

RULES FOR SPACING in the Calligraphic Mode:

1. Ultimately the eye is the judge for spacing. These rules should help, but the eye determines the space, depending on the width of the o chosen. The eye sees the patterns of white space made by the letters, and is only satisfied by an even distribution of space or color throughout the writing.

2. All spacing of lower case letters relates in some way to the width of the o or the parallelogram chosen.

3. In this GUIDE the width of the parallelogram is exactly one half the height for the calligraphic mode. IT IS RECOMMENDED that students discipline themselves to stick to this width for the calligraphic mode until they reach the last section of this book where several other spacings are illustrated.

4. Straight vertical strokes should be placed just to the right of the vertical Guide lines on the Guide Sheet "L" in the back of this book. Ellipses and elliptical curves should overlap the vertical guides slightly.

5. Adjacent straight vertical strokes are separated by the width of a space (full parallelogram), measuring from the left side of one stroke to the left side of the next stroke. ||

6. When a curve is adjacent to a straight stroke they are separated by approximately 2/3 of a space. |( )|

7. When two curves are adjacent, they are separated by approximately 1/3 of a space.)(

8. Spacing of c, s, v, w, x, and the right side of k follows the rules for curved letters because the eye takes into account the amount of space inside these letters and sees it as separation between them and the adjacent letters or, because of the greater amount of space inside these letters, does not require as much separation between them and the adjacent letters.

9. Spacing after r varies between one space and 1-1/3 spaces. Usually you will have to watch that you don't leave too much space after r.

10. If two ff's, two tt's, ft or tf appear, draw the two verticals first, then cross both with one stroke.

NOTE: The separations described above in 6, 7, 8, 9 are based on writing with a nylon-tipped pen in this section of the GUIDE. When an edged pen is used there may be a slight variation from these measurements but, if you learn them here, your eye will become accustomed to this even spacing.

T mint, minimum, unit, mill,

C →

T until, lint, hill, funny, nifty,

C →

T ıc time, untidy, manner,

C →

T helmet, hallelujah, many,

C →

T&C magnet · jet ·

Is your spacing even?

T goon, gear, eager, equal,

C →

T & C people · door ·

T garment, rent, general, ivy,

C →

T cocoa, small, corrupt, exit,

C →

T flivver, sessions, azure, wacky,

C →

Turn your writing upside down and check spacing and branching

T checkers, cool, grudge, rabbit,

C →

T khaki, prove, accord, read,

C →

T backwards, crawl, cogent,

C →

LISTS OF WORDS FOR SPACING PRACTICE

Easiest: two parallel straight strokes:
mint unit minimum nut hill limit until lint my him funny nifty lift fill muffin

Intermediate: one straight, one curved stroke:
time lentil manner hallelujah one many mat jam main manage bingo untidy magnet hat hanger magnolia loft left bill again agate golly night gelatin bib gamma magnanimity doubt date gauntlet jet

More difficult: two adjacent curves:
door genealogy gear keg adequate agog equal banjo equal before abbate egg hedge meant eager beautiful liberate jamboree people

Most difficult: mixed plus interior spaces:
checkers cool rent general garment grudge rabbit khaki prove accord corrupt session read flivver ivy backwards crawl bother niece cogent cocoa small catastrophe exam exit azure fix licorice wacky wax citation arrangement excellency breakfast citrus lick crawl concentrate concentric camera.

Project II

EDGED PEN – PEN ANGLE – ALPHABET WITH PEN

WARNING! DANGER! If you miss any of the important points in THIS lesson, all future practice of Italic will be wasted! of no value! And some day you will have to come back to this page and start all over again. NO OTHER one lesson in this book is as important as this one, for if you hold the pen correctly, it almost writes well automatically. If you hold it incorrectly, there is almost nothing you can do to make it write well!

For this project you will need a Broad pen (or broad oblique for left-handed writers); Guide Sheet 1 in the back of this book; white unlined writing paper, thin enough that the guide lines may be seen through the paper, 8-1/2" x 11" (the size of these pages), and paper clips.

ESSON 12: GETTING TO KNOW THE EDGED PEN AND PEN ANGLE

After filling your pen, touch it to the paper many times and see if you can get the ink to come out. IF the entire edge of the pen is not on the paper, you will not get ink, for the ink flows down the slit and along the edge of the pen. If only a corner of your nib is on the paper, no ink will flow. If you have a fountain pen and the ink doesn't flow immediately, you can drop it lightly on its tip on a piece of paper and force the ink through the nib. This is a sort of breaking in process that sometimes is necessary.

If you use a dip pen that has been packed in oil to preserve it, you can break it in by dipping and wiping it about four times until the ink forms an even, thin film on the surface of the pen.

Now move your pen around on a piece of paper and you will notice that when you move it along its thin edge you make thin strokes, if you move it along its breadth you make thick strokes, if you move it in a wavy ribbon, without turning the pen, you make a line of varying width. DO the above with your pen on your own paper. Here is what it might look like.

MOST IMPORTANT to Italic writing is learning the proper angle at which to hold the pen, and maintaining the pen always at that angle no matter where you are on the page. It is in this fundamental aspect of writing where many beginners fall down, failing to realize the importance of it, and failing to really master it before proceeding. READ CAREFULLY and UNDERSTAND the following instructions before proceeding!

The edged pen must always be held in the same position with its edge constantly at a 45° angle to the line of writing like this:

Left oblique nibs by left-handed writers like this:

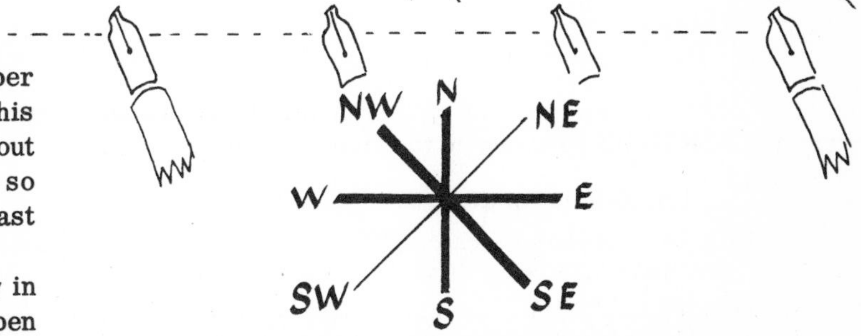

The full edge of the pen must be kept on the paper without pressure. A right-handed writer will have his arm crossing the paper at a 45° angle, his elbow out and his hand turned comfortably onto its right side so that he can barely see the tip of his little finger past the left side of his thumb.

A left-handed writer will usually have his elbow in and his wrist flat on the paper, depending on the pen and position he chooses. (See "Special for the Left-Handed" published by Italimuse, Inc. for all the possible positions, and examples of the writing of left-handed writers.)

IMAGINE a compass marking the directions on the map of your writing page. As you hold the pen correctly and lightly, and move it diagonally SW to NE / (or lower left to upper right) you will draw the thinnest lines possible with your pen. Notice that you must move the paper or move your arm as you cross the page in order to keep the pen in the correct position and keep the lines thin: Place your pen exactly over the drawing of a pen at the beginning of the line below. TRACE AND COPY the line, and see that when you reach the end of the line your pen is in position exactly over the drawing.

(For the left-handed writers the EDGE of the pen should line up with the EDGE of the pen in the drawings below.)

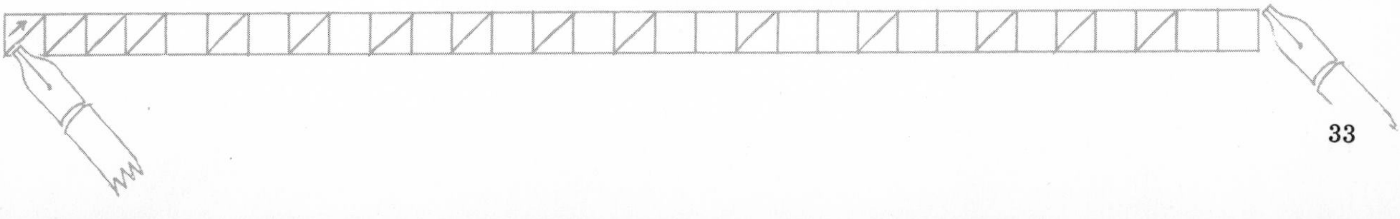

When you move the pen downward from NW to SE (or upper left to lower right) you will draw the thickest lines possible with your pen. Again, place your pen exactly over the drawing of the pen at the beginning of the line, and keep the angle as you cross the page so that your pen is in position exactly over the drawing at the end of the line.

(Try writing WITHOUT the pen cap on the shaft of the pen. It may help you have a lighter touch.)

Now, keeping your pen at the same angle, draw a plus sign. If your pen angle is correct the two strokes will be of equal thickness without turning your pen between strokes. If they are not equal, slant your pen and try again. Can you keep the two strokes even for the entire line? Move your hand and arm, but don't change the angle of your pen!

WATCH YOUR ELBOW! (Right-Handed Writers) Your elbow should be well to the right of your hand. As you move across the page your elbow will move off the paper (or pad or book) long before your hand reaches the right margin. In fact, if you are holding the pen at the correct angle, your elbow will already be off the right edge of the pad when you start writing the top line. Review the pictures of the writing position on page 16, noting especially the angle of the arm, position of elbow, and the turned position of the hand.

WATCH YOUR ELBOW! (Left-Handed Writers) Keep your elbows IN. Never let your elbow go beyond the left edge of the page, and never let your elbow be in a position to the left of your hand. Review the pictures of the writing position on page 16, noting especially the angle of the arm and the position of the elbow.

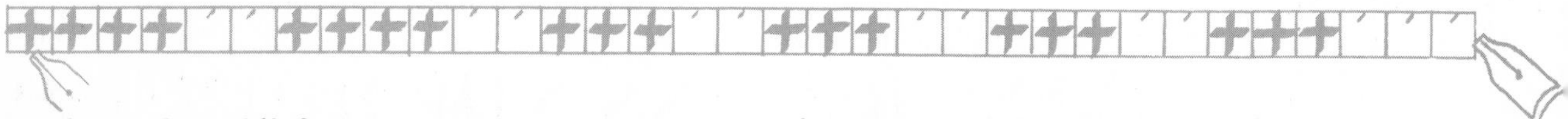

Now draw a box. All four sides should be of equal thickness if your pen angle is correct.

DO NOT let the edge of your pen tip towards one of the corners of the nib, or ink will not flow. Hold the pen lightly so you can feel that the whole edge of the pen is touching the paper.

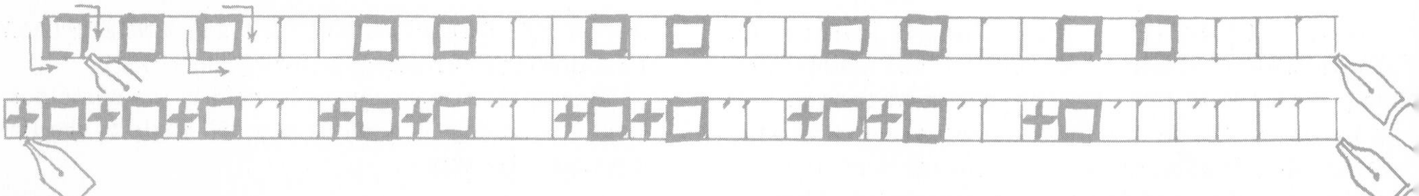

Now try holding your pen in the WRONG POSITION so that you can see what happens, and can later detect any errors in your pen angle.

First, make pluses and boxes with your pen in a too-flat position (as in the drawings). Notice which lines are thick and which lines are thin and see why.

Too flat:

Now turn your pen way up on end and make pluses and boxes with your pen in too steep a position (as in the drawings). Notice which lines are thick and which are thin and understand why.

Too steep:

Now once more slant your pen correctly, and make pluses and boxes with strokes of equal thickness.

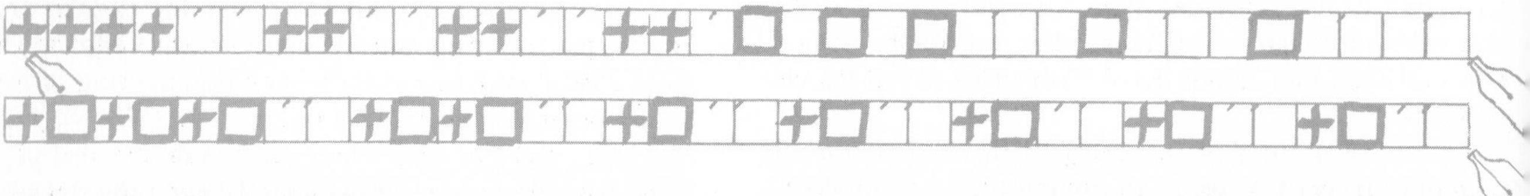

Now with your pen in the correctly slanted position make two pluses at the left side of the paper, two pluses in the middle of the page, and again two on the right hand side. Write one plus on the model and one right next to the model. Can you keep the arms of equal thickness at all three places on the page? It means moving your arm and hand, or the paper, without turning the pen.

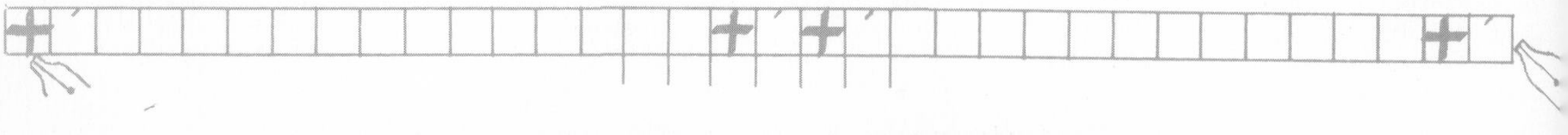

LESSON 13: LEARNING THE ALPHABET WITH CORRECT PEN ANGLE

KEEPING your pen slanted at the 45° angle shown in the drawings, TRACE AND COPY the following lines. Be sure to check your pen angle at the beginning and end of each line by drawing pluses and boxes with equal sides.

This matter of pen angle will have to be a very conscious part of your writing until the habit of keeping the pen in the right position is firmly established. Until that happens, there are key letters, described in numbers 1, 2, and 3 below, which you can continually use to check your pen angle.

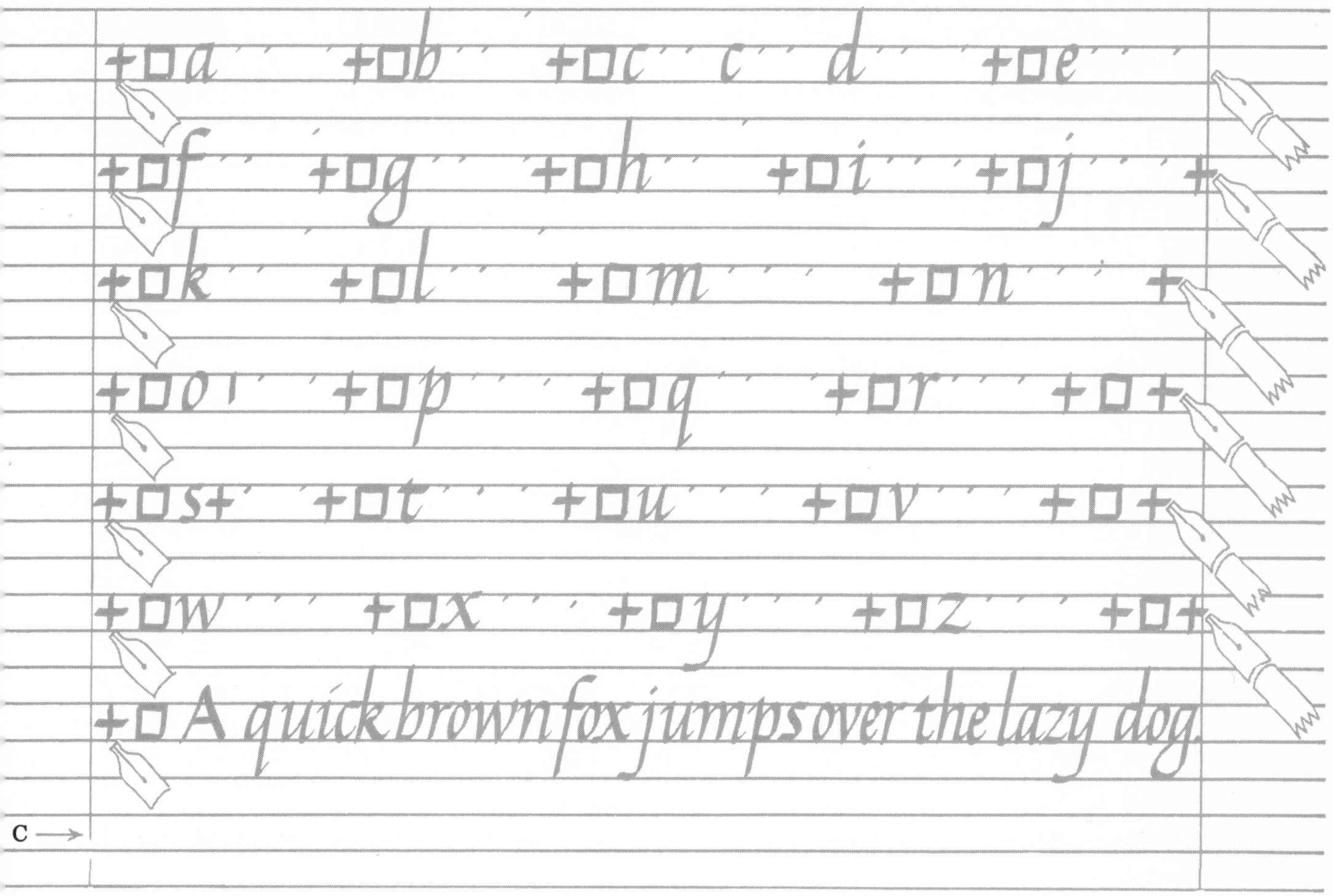

A quick brown fox jumps over the lazy dog.
C

1. The following letters all have horizontal and vertical strokes which should be of equal thickness

2. These letters should not appear thick or thin, and the 45° angle should be very apparent at the bottom of each stroke: Not or

3. The following letters have ascenders starting on the ascender line. At the top of each ascender you you should be able to clearly see a 45° angle: Not or

Now try these key letters with the WRONG pen angle so you will see how they look when the pen angle is incorrect.

First make pluses and boxes with TOO FLAT a pen, then trace and copy these letters with this too-flat pen-angle. Notice how fat the vertical strokes look; how hard it is to make narrow curves; how thin the horizontal parts of the letters are.

Too Flat

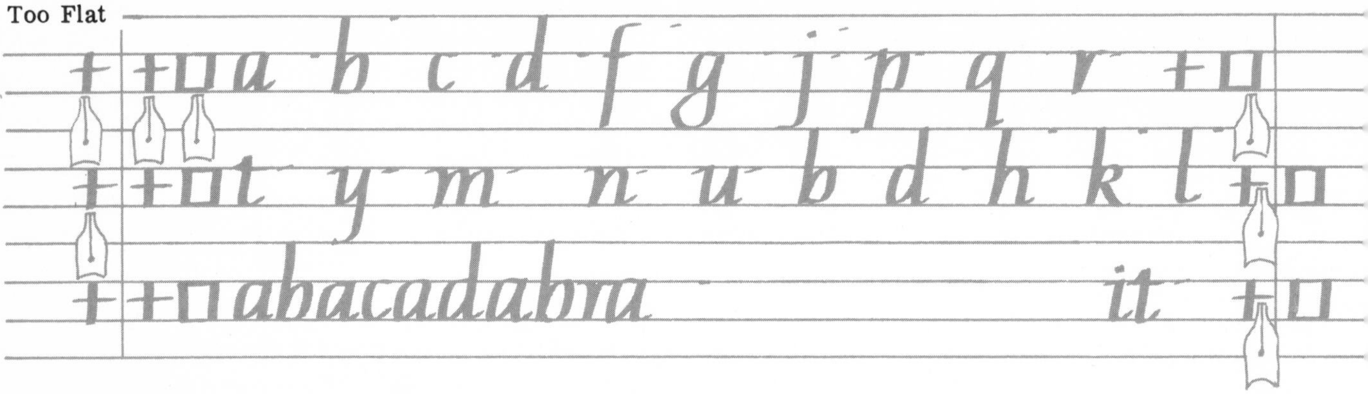

Now make pluses and boxes with TOO STEEP a pen, then trace and copy these letters with this too-steep pen angle. Notice how thin and scrawny the vertical strokes look; how spikey the narrow curves come out; how thick the horizontal parts of the letters are.

Too Steep

Notice how impossible it is to see the 45° angle at the top of the ascender letters in both of the above groups

Now practice these key letters with the CORRECT pen angle and enjoy the beautiful proportions of the letters

Correct Pen Angle

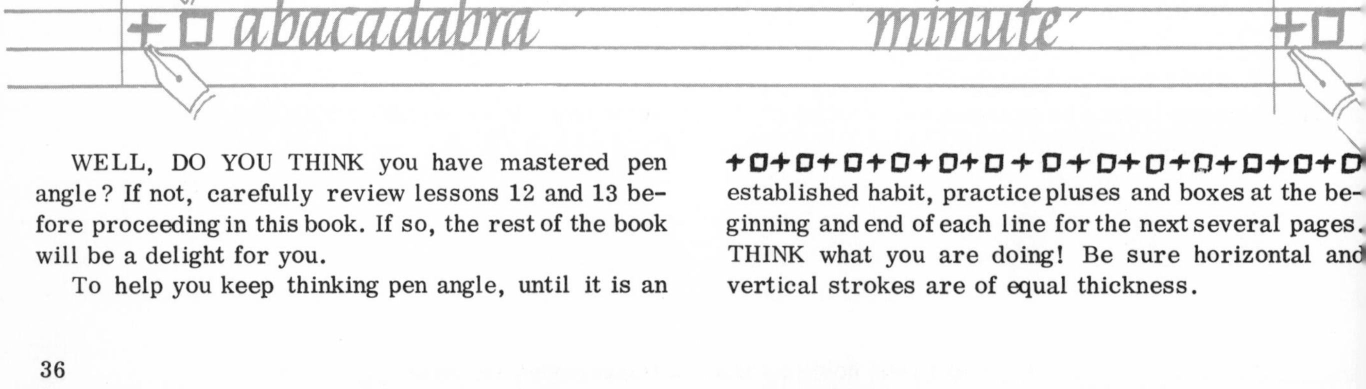

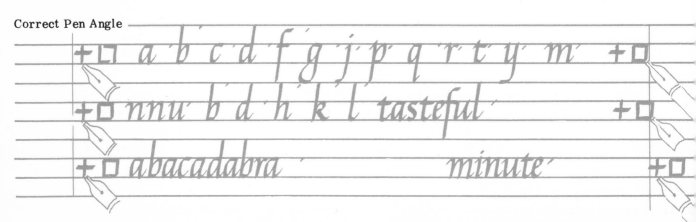

WELL, DO YOU THINK you have mastered pen angle? If not, carefully review lessons 12 and 13 before proceeding in this book. If so, the rest of the book will be a delight for you.

To help you keep thinking pen angle, until it is an +□+□+□+□+□+□+□+□+□+□+□+□+□ established habit, practice pluses and boxes at the beginning and end of each line for the next several pages. THINK what you are doing! Be sure horizontal and vertical strokes are of equal thickness.

ESSON 14: FAMILY LIKENESSES: a-shapes and inverted a-shapes

a, d, g, q, u, have this shape in common: . b and p contain this a-shape inverted and reversed: .

Remember the important points you learned about these letters. Make yours exactly like the model.

For all of your work from now on, write the date completed at the bottom of each page. Do the same thing when you copy a page on your own paper: Write the page number on your paper together with the date.

For this lesson and all of the following ones, trace the model and copy next to it while you are learning the new element presented in each lesson. When your copy looks very much like the model, STOP tracing and copying, and COPY ONLY on your own paper using the guide sheet numbered at the bottom of each page. Save the models and spaces for later review. An * indicates where you might stop tracing and begin copying.

aa aa dd dd gg gg qq qq

bb bb bb pp pp pp bp

bade, data, aggravate, billabong, compare,

acquaint explain apt

probable approach

principal, apparatus, propaganda, gauge,

fandango, bolero, palpitate, babble, barcarole,

ballade incomparable

agreeable euphony

cacophony approbate

LESSON 15: FAMILY LIKENESSES: Elliptical shapes and wedges
o, c, e, l, t have elliptical lower curves in common

NEW + jocose, violoncello, heliotrope, coconut, cocoon, □

→

* □ helicopter oratorio □+□+

+ choreographer concerto

These letters have white wedge-shapes in common:
Keep the wedges the same size.

mnhkrbpadgquy + □

NEW □ + breadth, among, mammal, had, piquantly, +

→

+ commander barracks □

* □ admirable rhapsody □+

+ magnify, denominator, engage, murmur, + □

→

□ hullabaloo harmonize +

+ □ communicate hard +□

□ ringing enharmonic +

+ □ harbinger abandon

Common Faults and Remedies I

MODELS	FAULTS	REMEDY
1. PEN ANGLE (p.a.)	Too flat atofr  Too steep atofm 	Study and practice pages 33 to 36 if you need to work more on pen angle
atofm 	Watch the verticals and horizontals in f t a a d g q b p . They should be equal in thickness if your p.a. is correct.	
2. BASIC SHAPES	Look at each model for the correct shape.	Review the first lessons
adgq	Here are some common errors that happen to this group Beginning push stroke: a (too long) a (not horizontal) a (too short Narrow curve: a (Too spikey); a (Too round) Parallel sides: a (Not parallel); a (Back-slanting) Lifting pen in wrong place: d d (Too soon) d (Not lifted at all—makes ascender thick) Ending strokes: a a a g g g g (ugly, clumsy)	
coe	Begin in the correct place: o e (o & e should begin with down strokes) Keep the elliptical shapes: c o e (Too skinny); o c e (Too fat) Lower curve: c e (Too sharp); c e (Too round) Loop of e: e e e (Too small); e e e (Too large)	
iu	i u (Serifs are wrong); u u (Narrow curve is missing); u (Sides aren't parallel)	
mnhkr	Branching: m n (Too high); m r (Too low) Elliptical arches: m n (Too round); m n n (Too spikey) Verticals; m n n (not parallel); Careless endings: m m m r r r k k	
bp	b (Pen should NOT be lifted); p p (Pen SHOULD be lifted & replaced at the base line) b p (Branching too low); b b p p (Sides not parallel) Narrow curve: b p (Too round); b p (Too spikey); b b p p (Bottom should be flat)	
ft	Cross stroke: f f t (Too low); f t (Too high); f f t (Not horizontal) f f t t (Length)	
s	s s (Two curves should appear the same size); s (Middle should be diagonal)	
vwyj	v r (End must turn in gently); v w (Too much slant); y j (No fishhooks).	
xz	x x z z z x z (Off balance); z (Too wavy); x (Keep the x)	

LESSON 16: FAMILY LIKENESSES: Horizontals, v-shapes, Review

These letters have horizontal strokes. Keep the horizontals HORIZONTAL!

NEW + □ a b c d f g j p q r s t x z □+ □

→

Watch the horizontals:

□ passed, class, passage, characterize, arabesque, +

→

+ surprise assist suppose □

+ □ staccato pizzicato if +

* □ feast, accept, across, jazz, saraband, sarcasm,

→

+ □ professor, scoffer, prestidigitator: juggler, + □

→

□ + extravaganza sport +

+ baseball ping-pong + □

□ cricket, rugby, football, softball, braggadocio, +

→

These letters have v-shapes. Be careful of the slant and the endings of these letters.

NEW + vary weaver vivacity □

+ wayward vivify verve □

□ + twirler vigor worry wry warrant viewer □ +

→

Remember these letters begin with sharp serifs: *ijptuy*

Remember these letters begin with narrow curves: *mnrvwx*

Remember these letters are the only ones written in two strokes: *d, e, f, p, t, x*

All the others are in one stroke. DO NOT lift your pen in the middle of one-stroke letters.

Remember, these letters end in narrow lower curves: *adhimnu*

These letters end in elliptical lower curves: *celot*

These words review all family likenesses. Try to remember every relationship between letters that you have been studying in the last pages.

+ heraldry breastplate buckler gauntlet armor □

→

□ helmet panoply moat +

+ gallant chivalry brave □

□ caparison adventure plucky castle defense rook +

→

+ barbican casement redoubt postern parapet □

→

→ □ invincible navigate □□ +

+ *vivacity, philosophy, baboon, appropriate,* □ + □

□ + *palpable, prospector, magnanimous,* □ +

+ *barge dingy scupper* + □

□ *starboard port bow* □ +

+ *gilding, gold, gesso, size, leaf, burnish, bright,* □

eggshell, hygroscopic, plaster, of, Paris, white, lead,

□ *parchment, vellum, glair, scissors, quill, scribe,* +

+ *scriptorium, knife, ink, sandpaper, weather,* □

□ + *damp, humid, illumination, silk, silver,* + □

ESSON 17: REVERSIBLES, COMPLETE ALPHABET, WEEKLY ALPHABET, QUOTATIONS

Trace and copy the first two lines, but copy the third, fourth and fifth lines on your own paper without tracing. Next, compare each letter carefully with the model and with "Common Faults" on page 39. Draw a line under the best letter in each group of three: your best a, best b, etc. Now place a check (✓) over each underlined letter which needs special work. . . any which does not look very much like the model. Then restudy the structure of the letters on pages 20 to 27; next dry-trace the model in the "Weekly Alphabet," that is, move your pen above the model without touching it. That will save the model for future study.

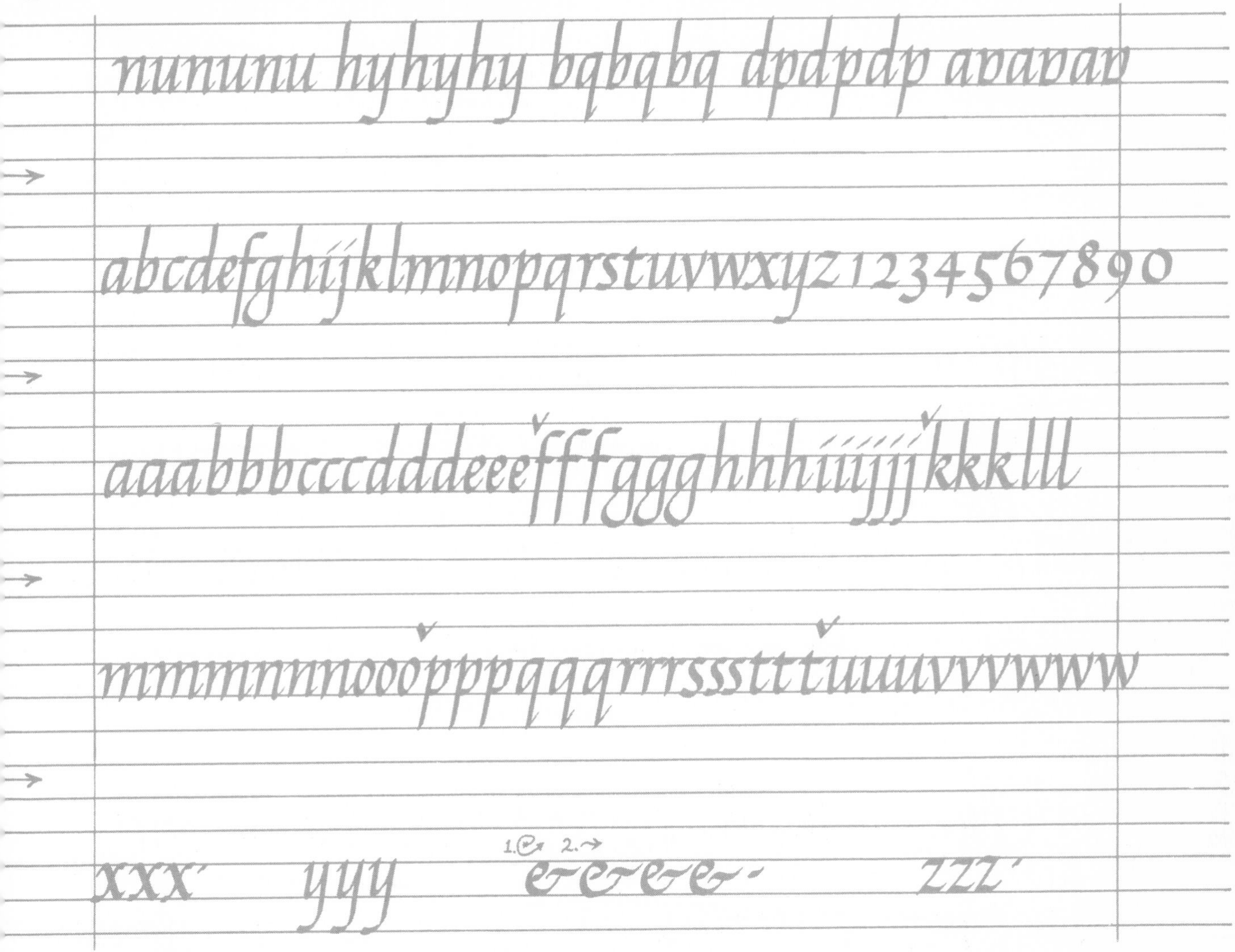

ERMANENT ASSIGNMENT:

Weekly Alphabet, From now on, every day write carefully five letters of the alphabet, each letter three times as above. On the first day write a to e, on the next day f to j, etc. Keep this work together on one sheet of paper, with the heading: "Weekly Alphabet." From now on this will give you a weekly record of your most careful, calligraphic alphabet. Compare with the models and Common Faults. Then give the villains (the bad letters) extra hard labor until they reform. Keep all of this weekly alphabet and special practice on one sheet of paper for each week.

One helpful way to give a difficult letter extra practice is to write an alphabet chain, using that letter between each letter of the alphabet: papbpcpdpepfpg, etc.

WEEKLY ALPHABET practice is by far the simplest way for the student and teacher to take stock of progress that is being made in the student's mental image or ideal of the model alphabet and his developing skill in drawing it. This is far easier than hunting through pages of work to find each letter of the alphabet. You can understand that it is difficult to have a perfect a every time you write one! But as the ideal image and skill in drawing it improve, as shown in the weekly alphabet, you can be certain of making progress in all of your writing. The weekly alphabet provides the simplest method for detecting any misunderstanding of the basic structure of the letters or any manual difficulty encountered. Once detected, the fault is easy to analyze and remove. When you work daily and faithfully on this Weekly Alphabet practice, consistent progress is assured.

QUOTATIONS:

Copy two of the following quotations, <u>each</u> on <u>half</u> a sheet of paper this size, using Guide Sheet No. 1a or 1b. Use simple block capitals.

Anything is possible — with practice

They fail, and they alone, who have not striven
Thomas Bailey Aldrich

Anyone can make excuses. But the success-
ful are those who overcome all temptations not
to work hard; they labor without complaint;
they get results

Work faithfully for eight hours a day and
don't worry. In time you may become the BOSS
and work twelve hours a day
and have all the worry

Excellence is produced by hard work, not by excuse

Project III

The Cursive Mode of Italic Handwriting

The purpose of this project is to learn the foundation for a rapid, cursive (joined and flowing), very readable and becoming handwriting with its roots in the Calligraphic Mode of Italic.

For this project you will again use the broad pen which you used in Project II, but you will use Guide Sheet 2 under your white paper.

ESSON 18: NEW SIZE, RHYTHM, JOINS

For speed, the hand must learn to join letters together in flowing rhythmic movements. Steps to speed are

1. Learning the joins
2. Becoming familiar with them in rhythmic movement
3. Gradually increasing speed (later on)

minimum

As you can see, it is not possible to join the letters in this word, keep the pen angle constant and keep the same spacing. The first m would join to the n, skipping the i, the n would joint to the second m, etc.

Now, reduce the size, keep pen angle and spacing the same and you can see that it is possible to join the letters with even spacing, although the proportion of width to height of the letters is changed:

minimum

Instead of the close spacing governed by the eye, the Cursive Mode will combine rhythmic movements with a horizontal thrust. The pen slides easily diagonally along its edge. The rhythm, the pen sliding diagonally and the feeling of horizontal thrust will set the spacing, keep the letter forms open and easy to read.

You will first learn joins to letters that are easiest to join and then proceed by steps to the more difficult. To get the feeling of rhythmic movement it is important to repeat the rhythm of a join or of a combination of letters in a word about three times.

You should TRACE AND COPY the model until you feel that you have it, then copy only on your own paper without tracing the model. Use Guide Sheet 2, and repeat each word three times. An asterisk (*) marks the places where the author feels you can start copying without tracing. The word "NEW" signifies new material which you should again TRACE & COPY.

GENERAL RULES FOR THE JOINING OF LETTERS:

1. Not every letter needs to be joined to its neighbor. Lifting the pen gives the hand a chance to relax and move on across the page.
2. The average number of connected letters that can easily be joined is three.
3. After learning all possible joins, the writer makes his own decisions about when to join and when to lift. BUT avoid the temptation to use no joins.
4. Diagonal joins should flow from a narrowly curving terminal, gliding along on the edge of the pen held at a 45° angle—the thinnest stroke possible when the pen is held correctly: *V* . They should not begin in a wide curve (*V*) or in a point (*V*).

Here is a list of possible joins which will be useful for reference after you have learned and practiced all of the joins.

TABLE OF JOINS

1. Diagonal joins may be made FROM these letters:

a c d e e h i k l m n u

2. Diagonal joins may be made TO these letters:

a c d e e g i j m n o p q r s t u v w x y

3. Horizontal joins may be made FROM these letters: *f o t*

and with special care from: *r v w*

4. Horizontal joins may be made TO any of these letters:

a c d e e g i j m n o p q r s t u v w x y

5. Joins are NOT made FROM descenders (*g j q y*); from push strokes (*b p s*); nor from x and z.

6. Joins are NOT made TO ascenders (*a b f h k l*) nor to z.

First, trace and copy the alphabet in the new width for the Cursive Mode:

abcdefghijklmnopqrstuvwxyz abcdefghij

FIRST CLASS OF JOINS (Easiest):
Joins with sharp upper angles to:

i j u o e e s t p v w y

Notice the peculiarities of joining to o, s, t, and both to and from e.

o, e, and s all begin with down-strokes after a join. Thus s loses its upper horizontal stroke, and o and e must have the tops added AFTER the first down stroke.

In the case of t, the join itself becomes the lead-in serif that begins t.

ııoooeeeeiieieieisssttttıoestoes

attest moist meet utter

As you make these joins and feel the rhythm, move easily and freely without drawing the letters so much as in the Calligraphic Mode. Keep o's, e's, m's and n's very open and full.

The conscious planning of spacing which is necessary in the Calligraphic Mode is replaced in the Cursive by naturally even spacing. This results from the rhythmic movement of the hand as it joins the letters diagonally at the 45° angle at which it holds the pen.

As you are practicing these pages in the Cursive Mode, remember to continue practicing the Calligraphic Mode: Weekly alphabet and words.

uuuuuu iuiu uouououo ueue

ususus utut upup uiui uyuy

uvuv uwuw ioio ieie ipip

iviv aiai aoao aeae asas

atat apap awaw cicici cococ

cece cscs dudu dodo dydy

hoho hehe htht hshs lele lolo lplp

* mimi meme nono eiei evev

etet eses evev ewew eeee eoeo

As you write in the Cursive Mode, do you feel the horizontal thrust?

juice bus diurnal brae asp

avenue cider cycle duty

hop highs might money

either jeopardy cockpit

eve new buy built riot live

SECOND CLASS OF JOINS (Intermediate):
Joins to curved entrances to: r n m x r n m x

EW irir inin imim ixix

urur anan cmcm cmcm drdr

dmdm lmlm mnmn erer enen

emem exex krkr knkn kmkm

firfir ninenine animosity

person far number flux

amen mnemonic exit

THIRD CLASS OF JOINS (Difficult):
Joins over the top and back again to: a a d g q

Don't lift your pen when joining over the top and back on these letters

EW iaia uaua aaaa caca dgdg

hqhq ldld nana mgmg kdkd

eaea ecec iqiq agag ncnc cqcq

egg iamb luau laager

can daisy hand lane lick
luck mail name each bad
kangaroo lapidary acme
* accept ashcan talc uncle
eccentric acid occident
funny jump keep laugh
business, made, ride, said, their, under, yeast, again,

→

eight him just kind light
make no please see up yes
them, best, can, hold, his, know, little, many, not, sing,

→

put these use any think
black blue green red orange
lavendar, must, beginning, basis, clear, mischievous,

→

peach madrigal dine her
announce conciseness and

Project IV

Capitals - Proportions - Simple Block Capitals

ENERAL RULES FOR CAPITALS:

1. The height of capitals is between the x-height and the ascender height.
2. Capitals look best upright, although with speed they may begin to slope a little.
3. When capitals only are used, there should be ample space between them.
4. Keep the 45° pen angle for now. Later we will vary this sometimes for capitals.

ESSON 19: ROUND CAPITALS BASED ON A CIRCLE
O and Q are full circles. C, G, and D follow the circle on one side, but the vertical of D and the terminals of C and G fall short of the other side of the circle.

Notice that in drawing O each corner of your pen forms a circle and the result is two interlocking circles. The effect of the edged pen held at the proper angle is an elliptically shaped white space inside. Note also that using the edged pen causes letters to overlap the square slightly at curves and angles. Trace and Copy these capitals. Use the order and direction of strokes shown. Keep the full width.

.W

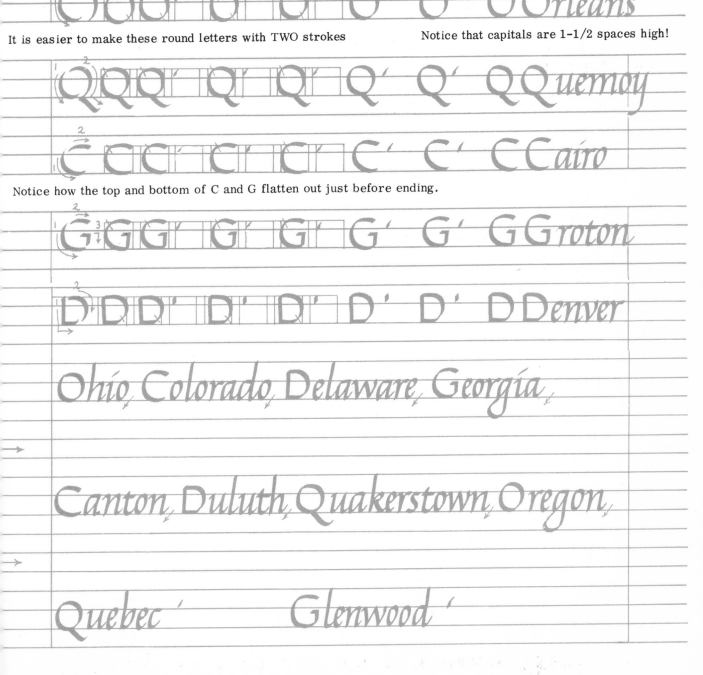

O O O O O O O O Orleans

It is easier to make these round letters with TWO strokes

Notice that capitals are 1-1/2 spaces high!

Q Q Q Q Q Q Q Q Quemoy

C C C C C C C C Cairo

Notice how the top and bottom of C and G flatten out just before ending.

G G G G G G G G Groton

D D D D D D D D Denver

Ohio, Colorado, Delaware, Georgia,

Canton, Duluth, Quakerstown, Oregon,

Quebec

Glenwood

GS1 = Guide Sheet 1

LESSON 20: RECTANGULAR CAPITALS 7/10 OF A SQUARE WIDE

These capitals fit into a rectangle 7/10 as wide as it is high.

NEW

H H H H H H H Harry

The horizontal of H and the point of K are just above center.

N N N N N N N Nathan

T T T T T T T Timothy

U U U U U U U Ursula

V V V V V V V Victor

The cross-stroke of A is just below center.

A A A A A A A Alexander

K K K K K K K Kenneth

X X X X X X X Xerxes

The white point of Y is right at center.

Y Y Y Y Y Y Y Ylburn (or y)

Z Z Z Z Z Z Z Zophar

* Alaska, Hawaii, Kansas, Nebraska, Arkansas,

→

Texas, Utah, Virginia, Xerguron, York, Ky., Nev.,

→

Zion Ala. Houston

NOT: A A A A A, H H H H, K K K, N N, T T T, V V, X X X, Y Y Y Y, Z Z Z

ESSON 21: NARROW CAPITALS 1/2 OF A SQUARE WIDE

These capitals fit into a rectangle 1/2 as wide as it is high.

NEW

L L L L L L L L L Leonard

E E E E E E E E E Edith

B B B B B B B B B Baker

F F F F F F F F F Felix

P P P P P P P P P Phyllis

R R R R R R R R R Robin

S S S S S S S S S Sandra

J J J J J J J J J J Judith

STOP - DETOUR - NO PASSING

Louisiana, El Paso, Burbank, Florida,

Rhode Island, South Dakota, Juneau,

ENTRANCE - ON STAGE - EXIT

NOT: L l, E E F, B B B B, F F, P P P, R R R, S S S S, J

LESSON 22: WIDE CAPITALS MORE THAN A SQUARE WIDE AND NUMERALS

The outer legs of M begin just inside the square and end just outside at the bottom.

The second and third strokes form a well-balanced V. The diagonals are NOT parallel.

NEW 1 2 3 4 M M M M M M M

Slightly sloping sides. NOT too much. NOT parallel diagonals:

→

1 2 3 4 W W W W W W

Really a double V, W does have parallel diagonals.

→

* Montana, Wyoming, Maine, Wisconsin,

→

Numbers must be easily distinguished

Horizontal stroke of 4 must cross the vertical

NEW 1 1 1 2 2 2 3 3 3 4 4 4

Trace and Copy these "New Style" numerals which are the same size as capitals

5 5 5 5 6 6 6 7 7 7 8 8 (8 or 8)

or like q in one stroke for speed in arithmetic.

8 9 9 9 q q q 0 0 0 0

8 and 9 are more beautiful in two strokes, but also practice them with 1 stroke for speed

* 1492, 1776, 1972, 1974, 1976,

→

1522, 1978, 1980, 1982, 1984,

→

5710 Main Street West 9876543210

→

NOT: M M (Spaces at bottom should be equal) M (parallel sides) M, W W, 1 2 3 4 5 6 7 8 9

LESSON 23: SPACING OF CAPITALS & NUMERALS

Spacing of capitals and numerals is by eye. The ideal is to have the total amount of white space between each letter equal. This is more difficult with capitals than with spacing in the calligraphic mode, for the round shapes and wide angles are more pronounced than in that compressed lower case alphabet.

Remember, as in our former discussion of spacing, two curved letters require less space between their closest points than two verticals as shown here:

DOHI

If we fill in these letters to make solid shapes, then we can more easily see the white space:

Notice that although D & O are closer than H & I, the total white area between them is the same. These three rules will help you get started. Then practice carefully, writing a word several times, improving the spacing each time.

1. The most space is required between two verticals: ||

IHIB IF HE

All of this area counts as space

2. The least space is required between two curves:)(

BOOM

3. Between angles and verticals, angles and curves, curves and verticals, the spacing is between these extremes \| \C |C

ABE LINCOLN

Give numerals plenty of room:

1776 vs. 1776

AABBCCDDEEFFGGHHIIJJKK

LLMMNNOOPPQQRRSSTT

UUVVWWXXYYZZ

IN 1842, 65 QUICK BROWN
FOXES JUMPED OVER
397 THIN LAZY DOGS

Quotations

1. I am only one, but I am one. I can't do everything, but I can do something. And what I can do, that I ought to do. And what I ought to do, by the grace of God I shall do. Edward Everett Hale

2. I resolved that I would permit no man to narrow and degrade my soul by making me hate him.
B. T. Washington

3. They that can give up essential liberty to obtain a little temporary safety deserve neither liberty nor safety. Benjamin Franklin

4. Face the situation fearlessly, and soon there will be no situation to face. Anon

5. Mirth is like a flash of lightning that breaks through a gloom of clouds and glitters for a moment; cheerfulness keeps up a kind of daylight in the mind, and fills it with a steady and perpetual serenity. Joseph Addison

6. All that stands between most men and the top of the ladder is the ladder. Anon

7. Great minds have purposes, others have wishes. Little minds are tamed and subdued by misfortune; but great minds rise above them. Washington Irving

8. The men who succeed best in public life are those who take the risk of standing by their own convictions.
J.A.Garfield.

9. In character, in manners, in style, in all things, the supreme excellence is simplicity. Longfellow

10. One of the best rules in conversation is never to say a thing which any of the company can reasonably wish had been left unsaid. Swift

11. The world turns aside to let any man pass who knows where he is going. Jordan

12. An irritable man is like a hedgehog rolled up the wrong way, tormenting himself with his own prickles.
Thomas Hood

13. Nothing is so contagious as enthusiasm... It moves stones, it charms brutes. Enthusiasm is the genius of sincerity, and truth accomplishes no victories without it. Bulver Lytton

14. When love and skill work together expect a masterpiece. Ruskin

15. It is a good and safe rule to sojourn in every place as if you meant to spend your life there, never omitting an opportunity of doing a kindness, or speaking a true word, or making a friend. Ruskin

16. He who wastes time in self-pity must tackle elephant by heels and pull out tusks. Eager

17. If everything is done with purpose in mind, it is not wasting time. Eager

18. Self is the only prison that can ever bind the soul.
Henry Van Dyke

19. I venture to suggest that patriotism is not a short and frenzied outburst of emotion but the tranquil and steady dedication of a lifetime. Adlai Stevenson

20. Let no one who loves be called altogether unhappy. Even love unreturned has its rainbow.
James Matthew Barrie

21. Therefore when we build... let it not be for present delight, nor for present use alone; let it be such work as our descendants will thank us for and... say..."See! this our fathers did for us." John Ruskin

22. Truth often suffers more by the heat of its defenders, than from the arguments of its opposers.
William Penn

23. All the ambitions are lawful except those which climb upward on the miseries or credulities of mankind. Joseph Conrad

24. First keep the peace within yourself, then you can also bring peace to others. Thomas A. Kempis

25. If you ride a horse, sit close and tight, If you ride a man, sit easy and light. Benjamin Franklin

26. Individuality is the salt of common life. You may have to live in a crowd, but you do not have to live like it, nor subsist on its food. Henry Van Dyke

27. Hear each man's counsel, but reserve thy judgement. Give every man thine ear, but few thy voice.
Shakespeare

28. If the Father deigns to touch with divine power the cold and pulseless heart of the buried acorn and to make it burst forth from its prison walls, will He leave neglected in the earth the soul of man made in the image of his Creator? William Jennings Bryan

29. The noblest charity is to prevent a man from accepting charity; and the best alms are to show and to enable a man to dispense with alms. The Talmud

30. Men grow only in proportion to the service they render their fellow men and women.
Edward V. Rickenbacker

31. He who does most, lives most. He who lives most, gives most. Edward V. Rickenbacker

32. Nothing that was worthy to the past departs—no truth or goodness realized by man ever dies, or can die. Thomas Carlyle

33. A success is one who decided to succeed—and worked. A failure is one who decided to succeed—and wished. William Arthur Ward

34. Never say, "Can't!" Say, "Not yet—but SOON, with practice." Eager

35. It isn't what you start that counts, it's what you finish. Anon

36. Look before you leap if you like, but if you mean leaping, don't look long. Anon

Project V

Review and Layout (Calligraphic Mode)
Join Studies Continued (Cursive Mode)

ESSON 24: QUOTATIONS. (Calligraphic Mode)
Write three quotations or sayings on three half-sheets of paper, centering each one. Use quotations from these pages or some favorites of your own. Choose quotations of different lengths. Use Guide Sheet 1.

Follow this procedure:
1. Choose the quotation (see pages 44 and 54).
2. Jot the quotation on scrap paper to determine what arrangement of words best brings out the meaning.

EXAMPLE: "Blessed are the peacemakers, for they shall be called the children of God."

Read each of the arrangements below and notice how b and d bring out the meaning of the quotation, and all other arrangements break up the meaning.

a. Blessed are the
peacemakers for they
shall be called
the children of God

b. Blessed are the peacemakers
for they shall be called
the children of God

c. Blessed
Are the peacemakers
For they
Shall be called the
Children of God

d. B L E S S E D
Are the peacemakers
For they shall be called
The children of God

e. Blessed are the peacemakers
for they
shall be called
the children of God

3. Next write your quote the size it will be, or just write the longest line. Center it on your paper (left and right). The point where the line falls on the left will be your left margin. If the longest line is centered, usually the entire quote or even a poem will appear centered unless some of the lines are much too short. If you decide on an uneven left margin, then you must adjust accordingly to make the piece appear centered.
4. Calculate the space the quote will occupy vertically and place it at the visual center (slightly above the actual center). To see how visual center is above the middle, write an s with even-appearing lobes, then turn the page upside down and look at it!
5. If you can draw concrete or abstract designs, you may enjoy arranging a quotation on paper in balance with such a drawing. NEVER do your lettering directly on a pattern or design, for it will detract from the design of the letters.

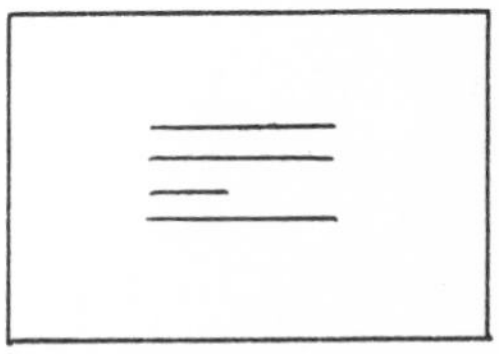

For a quote

For a poem

LESSON 25: JOIN STUDIES, CONTINUED (CURSIVE MODE) Guide Sheet 2.

FOURTH & FIFTH CLASS OF JOINS (Horizontal to easiest and intermediate). Joins to:

e i o p t u v w y; n m r

NEW

oioi oeoe ojoj oooo opop osos otot

ouou ovov owow oyoy oror onon om

fifi fefe ffff fofo fsfs ftft fufu fyfy

titi tete tjtj tsts twtw tyty oiloil

* *hood soja moon lop lose*

not ifs bout over wow boy final feet fjord forget

→

time tear bootjack fits tube

footwork empty nitwit from ore on bomb fox true

→

SIXTH CLASS OF JOINS (Horizontal to difficult) Joins to: *a c d g q*

NEW

fafa oaoa ococ ogog oqoq tata tctc

far far oath oath octave octave

* *odd odd log log baroque baroque*

tail tail itch fast to down

ton truck before does doodle fat today monotony

→

Don't try to make the pen write the letters. Hold it lightly and LET it write.

The Swans

Slowly seven swans
float down from the sky
and lighting on the bronze
surface of the inlet, they
sail in solemn procession,
seven white half notes
on the rippled staff
of the dark bay.

Milton Kaplan

LESSON 26: COPYING A SHORT POEM (Calligraphic Mode) Guide Sheet 1

Copy this short poem, or another of your choice, utilizing what you have learned about layout in the writing of a quotation in Lesson 24.

LESSON 27: JOIN STUDIES, CONTINUED (CURSIVE MODE)

SEVENTH CLASS OF JOINS (Doubles with horizontal joins):
In doubles involving t and f, write the two verticals first, then the horizontal which joins to a following letter.

oo ff tt ft tf

NEW

oopoop oosoos oot oov tti tte

tto tts tty fte fto fts ffi ffu ffe

ffa ffo ffs ffn ffr tta fts fte

* *hoop boost foot groove attic*

mitten, butter, bottom, butts, witty, after, leftover,

softspoken, nifty, diffuse, buffet, buffoon, offset, affair,

EIGHTH CLASS OF JOINS (Tricky)

Joins from: *v w r*

Great care must be used with these joins. With care they may join to all the letters in classes 1 to 6. The r must branch high enough so it will not be confused with v. The r-join should dip slightly to aid readability.

NEW

ri re ra rs ro ru vi ve va vo vu

rib, rigor, vigor, rim, vim, rat, vat, rumor, rude, river,

* *rally rutabaga vacuum*

van ran variance velvet

verify vernal vertebrate

very, viceroy, wilderness, wives, wring, wreck, bowery,

No man is an iland intire of itselfe
Every man is a peece of the Continent
A part of the Maine,
If a clod bee washed away by the sea
Europe is the lesse,
As well as if a Promontorie were;
As well as if a Mannor of thy friendes
Or of thine own were:
Any man's death diminishes me,
Because I am involved in mankind
And therefore never send to know
For whom the bell tolls
It tolls for thee

John Donne

ESSON 28: REVIEW CALLIGRAPHIC AND CURSIVE MODES

Copying a quotation provides interesting practice where you can concentrate on the letter-forms, joins and spacing.

Copy this quotation on white paper in the Cursive Mode (as illustrated), using Guide Sheet 2. Then copy it again in the Calligraphic Mode, using Guide Sheet 1 (without joins).

But it was not its size that now impressed my companions; it was the knowledge that seven hundred thousand pounds in gold lay somewhere buried below its spreading shadows. The thought of the money as they drew nearer, swallowed up their previous terrors. Their eyes burned in their heads; their feet grew speedier and lighter; their whole soul was bound up in that fortune, that whole lifetime of extrav-agance and pleasure, that lay waiting there for each of them.

from "Treasure Island"
by Robert Louis Stevenson

Copy this quotation on white paper in the Calligraphic Mode as illustrated, using Guide Sheet 1. Then copy it again in the Cursive Mode, using Guide Sheet 2.

Now We're Writing...

Project VI

Using the Medium Pen

In this project you will review the alphabet and learn to use the medium pen which is the most commonly-used size. Remember, the nib should be square for right-handed writers and either left-oblique or left-handed for left-handed writers.

LESSON 29: THE MEDIUM PEN AND SMALLER WRITING in Calligraphic and Cursive Modes

The following exercise presents nonsense words invented for pleasure and contributed by Carl W. Meyer. The use of these words and other unusual, unfamiliar passages in this book are to encourage the student to look at the model more frequently than he would when copying completely familiar words and passages. Always copy carefully, trying to make your copy look exactly like the model as possible.

Notice, as letters are smaller, the width also is narrower proportionally

CALLIGRAPHIC MODE with Medium Pen. Use Guide Sheet 3

T abcdefghijklmnopqrstuvwxyzabcdefghijklmnopqrstuvwxyz

C →

T fyceraque oi timre uametry su romd dillgrode subbigum

C →

irrinupted ganforthy likimpotest klip occaptar currumly

octobanal queamish ruawyme whiark twaftonum ol tift

duss frint orf fringale mune soyame slubborgan simplural

oypanistery ud worsignabure gur tift havekut plang deselk

CURSIVE MODE with Medium Pen. Use Guide Sheet 5 with the smaller spacing

T abcdefghijklmnopqrstuvwxyz fyceraque oi timre uametry

C →

uametry evrahust sarf nolk diaferes su romd dillgrode pelled

spandole subbigum frint irrinupted ganforthy likimpotest

occaptar currumly octobanal queamish ruawyme whiark klip

twaftonum ol tift duss frint orf fringale mune soyame deselk

Is your hold on the pen relaxed?

ESSON 30: CAREFUL COPYING OF SHAPES—SPACING—JOINS

Copy the first half of the page in the Calligraphic Mode with Guide Sheet 3. Copy the second half of the page in the Cursive Mode with Guide Sheet 5. Trace if you like.

are walk better clean drink found hurt may warm sixten four

were ask big come from me one read will stop have upon wish

ate bring could funny run work much sleep here sense receive

occasion separate receive column would away running past

unusual amphibian minute consummate imagery write

inimitable yellow magenta violet ultramarine cut ballast

enchantment recognize question must apprehension want

optimist explain jocundity famulus gasoline octane proponent

joker zealot promontory isthmus aboard brigantine galley

weather skipper stowaway marooned abandon buoyancy your

grinning laughing smiling beaming bright glowing sparkling

radiant shining bemused genial gleeful hourly noon night

elegant prophecy was small occupation stop went daily weekly

fortnightly monthly bimonthly quarterly semi-annual annual

biennial decenial centuple bicentenary millenial dawn dusk

dayspring midday afternoon sunset twilight dusk evening

Do not copy at one time all of the words on this page! Use them in your daily warm-ups or for joining practice, or later for speed work. As you do this type of work with these words, write each word more than once to find the rhythm of the word and build the habit of rhythm into your hand. Alternate short words with long words. Place a check above words which you have used so you can quickly find new words the next time.

an air anon admit animal account anterior me ace main anvil hammer anemone handsome am mum acme humor anthem measure admonish in hum done minim cannon hundred ancestor ha any name angry homing command maintain as ham anna mouse amount numeral dominion hi ant mime amuse nation amiable humanity ad man aunt manner common honour announce my aim hail adage minute avocado monogram ay mat ahem hence accent mundane accident at hag dear mummy banana humming behemoth ho den hair under murmur ancient monument do not cone honey acacia nominal dominoes he mud come human adhere meander alphabet ax hid acid money summer nothing ignoramus he lay hind haunt among manual include macaroni amphibious em hut inch harem pamper handful appetite momentary en mug lead munch accept morning notation automobile us men idea maple sugar apache macabre neighbor commandment up hat game manna active minimum medieval or nap lamb motel across morning habitual diminuendo manufacture lo cat moon annoy napkin archery mechanic necessary is nag liar never avenue machete hesitate microscope aw mop ugly madly appeal meddle beautiful millionaire ma day neon male again altar female la eat camp amber nickel appoint or met help minus hamlet mystery moccasin handiwork to nip hump music nuclear military harlequin manipulate mut home night mirror heroine nuisance mop hide north museum herself merchant meteorite afar ahoy able arch away axis axle atop avid avow lawn leap into limb ugly ankle amble aside astir atlas ditch afire apace acorn apply acute apron argue after light joins sunny funny gnome attic avast avoid await awake until unite apathy absent awkward adamant average mut may mix mob mop maul moan mean made mail make mare mark meet mast mate meek melt memo meow mesh mess mica mien mild mile mill mint miss mist mock mode mold mole mood more moss most moth move much mule mute myth major manila march melon merry meter midst might mirth moral mouth muddy monster minute memory manage manner mammal middle female mallet mantle margin mature medley mellow melody mingle misery modify molten moment monkey motion muscle muting mutual myself minuet middle message mistake moisten mortify mystify mathematician mimeograph machinery melodrama metaphor millionaire mischief mountain multiply hey hay hit hop hot how hug hack haft half halo halt harp haul heir hep herb herd here hero high hike hill hive hoax hold hole holy home hook hood hoop horn hose hour howl huff huge hull hung hurl hurt habit halve heavy hello hinge horse hovel hurry hymnal homing humane honest homage handle harden heaven heckle height herald hermit hither hooray huddle hunch hunger hunter hungry however handkerchief net new nod nary nine none nice nail navy near neat neck need nest next nose note noun numb nasty naval nerve night noise nomad noose notch novel narrow native nature nebula needle nephew nibble nimble noodle notice notion noncom neglect neither notable omnipresent contemplation monomania momentum immense commencement murmur communication enumeration matrimony finis

WORDS FOR SPACING PRACTICE IN EITHER MODE

In practicing these words, write each one several times until you feel it is the best possible spacing that you can give it.

accent accordance affix ancient alkaloid accomodation amaryllis amethyst animate annual appetizer approximate assembly audience audacious authorize axillary auxiliary axis axle azurite axe blizzard boxcar buffalo buzzer buzzard cabinet caddy calligraphy candidacy cardinal carrousel cerfix catalogue citadel citric acid chaffinch chameleon checker chiffon cheerful chromium cocoa computation coffee colorful concerto commemorative concentric congress corona cocoon cosmonaut eccentric ecology ego economics corsage coxswain cranberry crazy credo cucumber daddy tintype desert display divided didactic dodge doldrum drum doodle dollar didactic doughnut drizzle duplex economy economies eagle eccentric economic effect efficiency effect elementary elfish emanate emancipate eminence empyrean ennoble expression enjoy entity enterpreneur extra extravaganza fledgling flibbertigibbet flocculent fluorescent fastidious feminine fisticuff fixative fizzle flourish flour fleecy fulfilled gimcrack giraffe gorge gourmet griffin grizzly bear guerrilla guest guess ham hallelujah haphazard harmonize harpsichord hazard hippopotamus hitchhike hocus-pocus homology huff homogenize homonym horizontal howitzer humbuggery humility hullabaloo humoresque hydroxide hyperbole hummingbird husbandry hydroplane hyperbola lofty hypothesis individuality integrity intelligence jocundity jiffy jinx jubilee landlocked lofty legerdemain licorice lithography limitations philosophy paleography local locomotive lozenge luxurious luncheonette lummox lugubrious luxuriant mademoiselle bubble magniloquence magnificent mathematics mazurka memorization middlemost maximum millenium monkey ostrich millipede mimicry mimosa mineralize minuteminder minuteman minimum maximize miscellaneous nobly minuscule mnemonic modulate modulation monotonous monochrome muffled multitude nebulous nobility ocean obelisk oblique perplexity periwinkle pixy perplex cox please plexus polarize pomegranate express reflect recurrent ruffle ruffian remembrance shoefly shuffle waffle billabong billion quadrillion sextillion shellfish stabilize stuffed summarized submaxillary sufferable sextant syllabilization official syntax offensive taffeta telltale mixable textile taffy texture twixt vexedly oxen hilarity exhilaration exasperation exchange executrix wizard magazine zipper exercise exclaim buff affluence

Daily-Weekly Routine Assignment

As you begin to write more freely and rapidly, you will encounter certain problems. Letters tend to lose their ideal shapes and the letters which branch (m, n, k, r) tend to lose their elliptical shoulders and become spikey. To counteract these tendencies and build a beautiful, fluid handwriting, it is wise to set a routine for daily and weekly work in addition to following the rest of the assignments in this book.

ILY WARM-UP PRACTICE (5 days a week minimum)
Practicing a "weekly-alphabet" in the calligraphic mode will give the hand review in the ideal letter shapes. A daily warm-up will give the hand special practice in arches; will help to build rhythm and fluency; and is an important step to building a rapid, beautiful, readable handwriting. Extra practice on your faults (certain letters, pen-angle, joins, spacing, or whatever they may be. See pages 39, 66, and 67) will make your writing more even.

USE the Special Warm-Up Guide Sheet on page 113. Later you may dispense with the guide lines.

1. On the first day the weekly alphabet includes the five letters, a to e. Write each letter three times (in the Calligraphic Mode) and underline the one letter of the three which you think you have written the best. To help you choose, analyze your letters and compare them with the models on page 62. On the following day you will use the next five letters of the alphabet.
2. On the next line after the weekly alphabet segment practice arches.
3. Pairs of m's joined together, thus adding counter-clockwise movement to the predominantly clockwise.
4. mumu increases the counter-clockwise movement.
5. For each of the following two lines, choose a word from page 64 (these contain m, n, h, k, or r and i, a, d, g, q, or u) and write it in the Cursive Mode, keeping the branching high. Write a check (✓) above the places where you have branched too low. On the following days you will use different words for lines 5 and 6.
6. For the next several lines give extra practice to faults which seem to persist in your writing (See pages 39, 66 and 67).

ALWAYS place the date by your Daily Warm-up to record your practice.

PUT all five daily Warm-ups on one sheet of paper.

WEEKLY MINIMUM PRACTICE

To make satisfactory progress in Italic Handwriting, you should plan to do faithfully the following work each week, spending fifteen to thirty minutes a day:

1. Daily warm-up and extra practice on faults.
2. Lesson Assignments (working in this book).
3. Two poems or excerpts of your own choice from other sources.
4. School-work or other writing.
5. Speed Practice (Daily after reaching page 75)
6. Self-grading of one of your poems each week (See page 67).
7. Keep track of your work on the Check List and Writing Record, page 109. Pick a certain day of the week to take stock. Every week on that day look over your work for the week, and mark your self-criticism on the Check List and Writing Record.

DAILY WARM UP SAMPLE

First Day

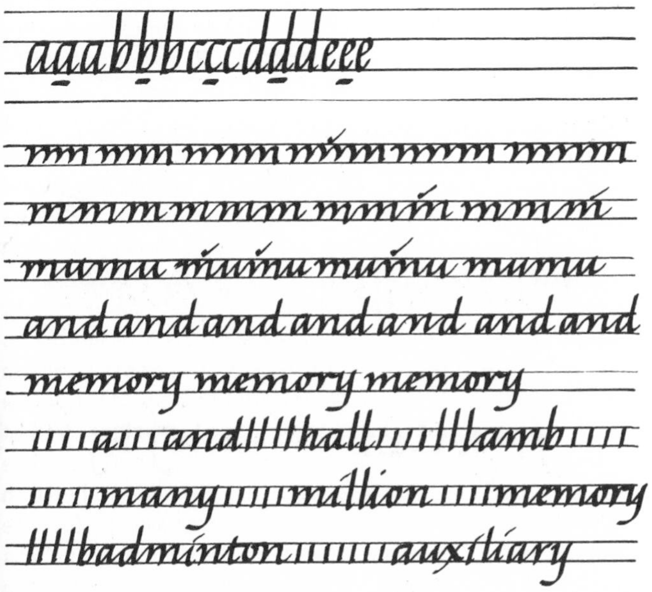

Second Day

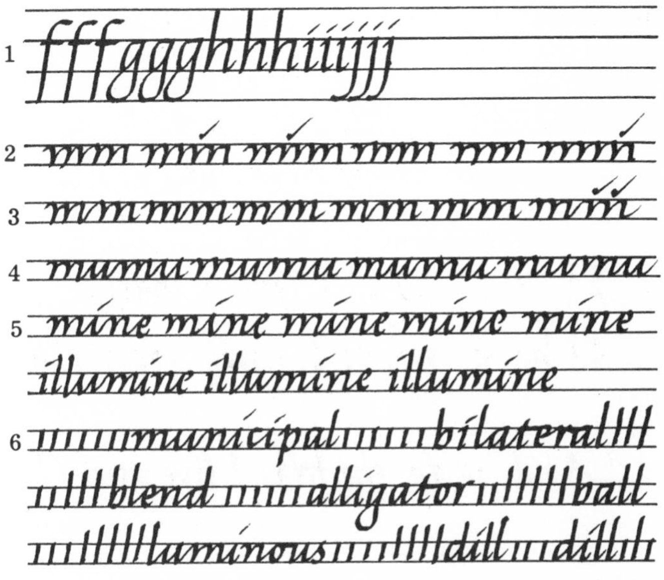

his Daily Warm-up is based on exercises recommended by Alfred Fairbank, Lloyd J. Reynolds and Arnold Bank

Common Faults and Remedies II

3. SLANT: An inconsistent slant produces writing like this: *hallelujah* . Another fault of verticals which hurts the slant on a page is called "wind-swept" or "banana-shaped" or "hooked" ascenders like these: *l l l l* . The same faults may occur in descenders like *p j y* . Any of these faults hurts the appearance of a page. To check your slant, use a ruler to draw lines through the verticals. Place your page over the Slant-detector Guide Sheet (page 111) to determine the degree of your slant. It should be between 5° and 10° for the Calligraphic Mode and between 5° and 15° for the Cursive Mode. *Draw lines through the verticals*

REMEDY:

1. Use Guide Sheet 3 or 4 under white paper. Practice parallel vertical strokes, gradually increasing the size. Make sure that they slant forward: *ııııııı|||||||||||*
2. Write *bldlflhlklllbldlflhlklbl* etc.
3. Write *mailmbilmcilmdilmeilmfilmgilmhil* , on through the alphabet.
4. Write *ıııımoneyıııııı animal ıııllhammerı* etc., using different words containing m and n.
5. If you tend to back-slant or have excessive forward slant, try slanting your paper at a different angle.
6. Back-slant is usually caused by too much thumb-pressure. Relax your thumb!

4. ALIGNMENT–SIZE: *animals water*
When tops and bottoms of letters are not even, the page acquires a dizzy, uneven look.

REMEDY:

1. Practice the alphabet sentences on page 76. Write carefully between double lines with a Guide Sheet, concentrating on the two lines, making the letters slightly overlap them, top and bottom.
2. If you tend to go up (or down) always, adjusting the slant of the page you write on may help you.

5. JOINS: *animal* . These rounded joins slow you down too much. *animal* . These joins which are too sharp tend to crowd the writing and make it hard to read. Joins should spring up directly in a narrow curve or speed will never be gained. Joins should be along the 45° edge of the pen:

REMEDY: Practice *ıuıuıu ıuıu ai ıuıuiua ia* , joins on pages 46 to 48 and joins in the words on page 64.

6. SPACING: *anima l* Slant, alignment and spacing are the most important factors in giving a page an even appearance. To check your spacing, draw lines through the verticals of *abdfghijlmnpqrtuy* , through the middle of *ceosvxz ceosvx* , and two equally spaced lines through *k* and *w* .
abcdefghijklmnopqrstuvwxyz abcdefghijklmno
If your spacing is good the lines should be about an equal distance apart, but check the rules on page 29 for the variations. Keep the space of o between words. Too much space between words tends to pull the writing apart, and the horizontal flow of the reading eye is interrupted by the vertical white rivers running through the writing.

REMEDY: With your broad pen and later medium pen repeat the progressive spacing exercises on pages 29 to 32. Carefully follow the instructions in the first paragraph on page 29. Then apply them to the words in the second column on page 64. Practice alphabet chains with m, n, h between each letter: ambmcmdmem, etc.

Find and list by number the most outstanding faults in these examples of students' work. Check your criticism with that listed at the bottom of page 67. Several have more than one fault.

1. *So it is now I am a man,*
so be it when I shall grow old,

2. *And so do the folks I live under!*

3. *drumming* 4. *How sweet is the*

5. *mhmimjm* 6. *fashion*

7. *forgotten* 8. *lofty hill*

9. *she l led peas* 10. *full*

Summary of Standards for Italic Handwriting

The abbreviation symbols listed for each fault will aid the teacher in marking papers.

STANDARD	DESCRIPTION	Abbrev. Symbol	Possible Score
1. PEN-ANGLE:	-15 for incorrect pen angle. The thinnest parts of your letters should be in these corners: o a n. Horizontal and vertical strokes should be equal: a t f. NOT: oatmlf (flat pen); or oatmfts (steep pen)	p. a.	15
2. BASIC SHAPES:	o not O ; a not a a ; t not t (See pages 39 & 53). -1 for each incorrect letter of the alphabet: if a's are wrong, -1; g's, -1, etc. (Circle the miscreants)	(a)	25
3. SLANT:	Not too much (no more than 15° for Cursive, 10° for Calligraphic); Never backslant mai, but consistent: mlilm, not: A m lC . Use page 111. -1 for each line of writing with poor slant.	////	20
4. ALIGNMENT:	Tops and bottoms of letters should be even. The size should be right. NOT: tops and bottoms -1 for each uneven line of writing.	=	10
5. JOINS (Cursive only):	Diagonal: an ai ; NOT an ai ai ; -5 if Too sharp: V. Horizontal: ti fi on rn vn wm -5 if Too round: U. No joins after descenders: yo ga or before ascenders: ab all -10 if No joins: nj. Exceptions: tt , or others when writing with speed: th all	V / U / nj	10
6. SPACING:	Space between verticals should be about equal. Space between words should be the width of 'o'. More space than that leaves white paths running through the page; less space causes illegibility. Space between lines of writing should be enough so that descenders of one line won't conflict with ascenders in the next.	Betw. verticals: # ; Betw. words: #| ; Betw. lines: #	10
7. APPEARANCE:	A general, artistic, neat appearance and legibility; a pleasant arrangement on the page; and an appeal to the eye are the important features in good handwriting.	Appear.	10

TE YOUR WRITING, one page every week. Write a column of numbers from 1 to 7 down one side of a page. Take each standard, one at a time, and look over your page. See how many points you can award your writing for each standard. For BASIC SHAPES, check your weekly alphabet with the model. You may wish to mark your mistakes with the symbol abbreviations shown. Give yourself 10 points for good joins and 10 points for good spacing in the Cursive Mode only. Since there are no joins in the Calligraphic Mode, allow 20 points for spacing when judging your work in that mode. Keep track of your faults on the Check List and Writing Record, page 109, and give them extra practice.

FOR CORRECTION OF FAULTS in pen-angle or basic shapes, see page 39. For correction of the remaining faults, see page 66.

abcdefghijklmnopqrstuvwxyz abcdefghijklmnopqrstuvwxyz

ABCDEFGHIJKLMNOPQRSTUVWXYZ

Answers to problems on page 66: 1:5,6 2:4,5,6 3:3,4,5,6 4:4,6 5:3 6:3,4,6 7:3,4 8:3,5 9:3,6 10:3

When I would know thee – my thought looks
Upon thy well-made choice of friends and books.
Then do I love thee, and behold thine ends
In making thy friends books, and thy books friends
Epigram 86 – Ben Jonson

Do what you feel to be right;
say what you think to be true
and leave with faith and patience
the consequences to God
F. W. Robertson

Whatsoever things are true, whatsoever things are honest,
whatsoever things are just, whatsoever things are pure,
whatsoever things are lovely, whatsoever things are of good report;
if there be any virtue,
if there be any praise,
think on these things.
St. Paul to the Philippians

LESSON 31: Center each of these quotations on its own piece of paper. Use Guide Sheet 3 or 4 and the Calligraphic Mode for the first two and Guide Sheet 5 or 6 for the third quotation in the Cursive Mode.

Project VII

Simple Roman Capitals

SSON 32: No matter what you do with capitals, now or ater, the essential forms you learned in the Block Capitals must be there. These Simple Roman Capitals appear to be dressed-up versions of Block Capitals. They approach the appearance of the Classic Roman Capitals which have served as a standard for capitals since the First Century A.D.

The pen-angle for Roman Capitals is usually flatter—about 15°. But watch for the places where it changes to 45° for the diagonals, and still steeper than 45° for certain vertical strokes in M and N. Roman Capitals should be upright.

TRACE and COPY one letter, then practice it on separate paper. Then the next letter, and so on. Use Guide Sheet 3.

Pen Angle:

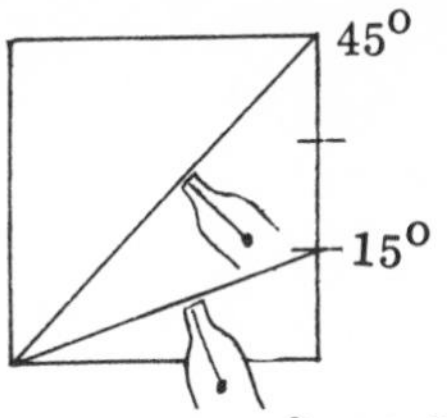

45°
15°

1
2
3

1. Pen angle begins at 45° and flattens as it curves out at the bottom for the serif.
2. Pen angle is 45°, flattens for the serif and cross-stroke. Simply turn the pen in your hand.

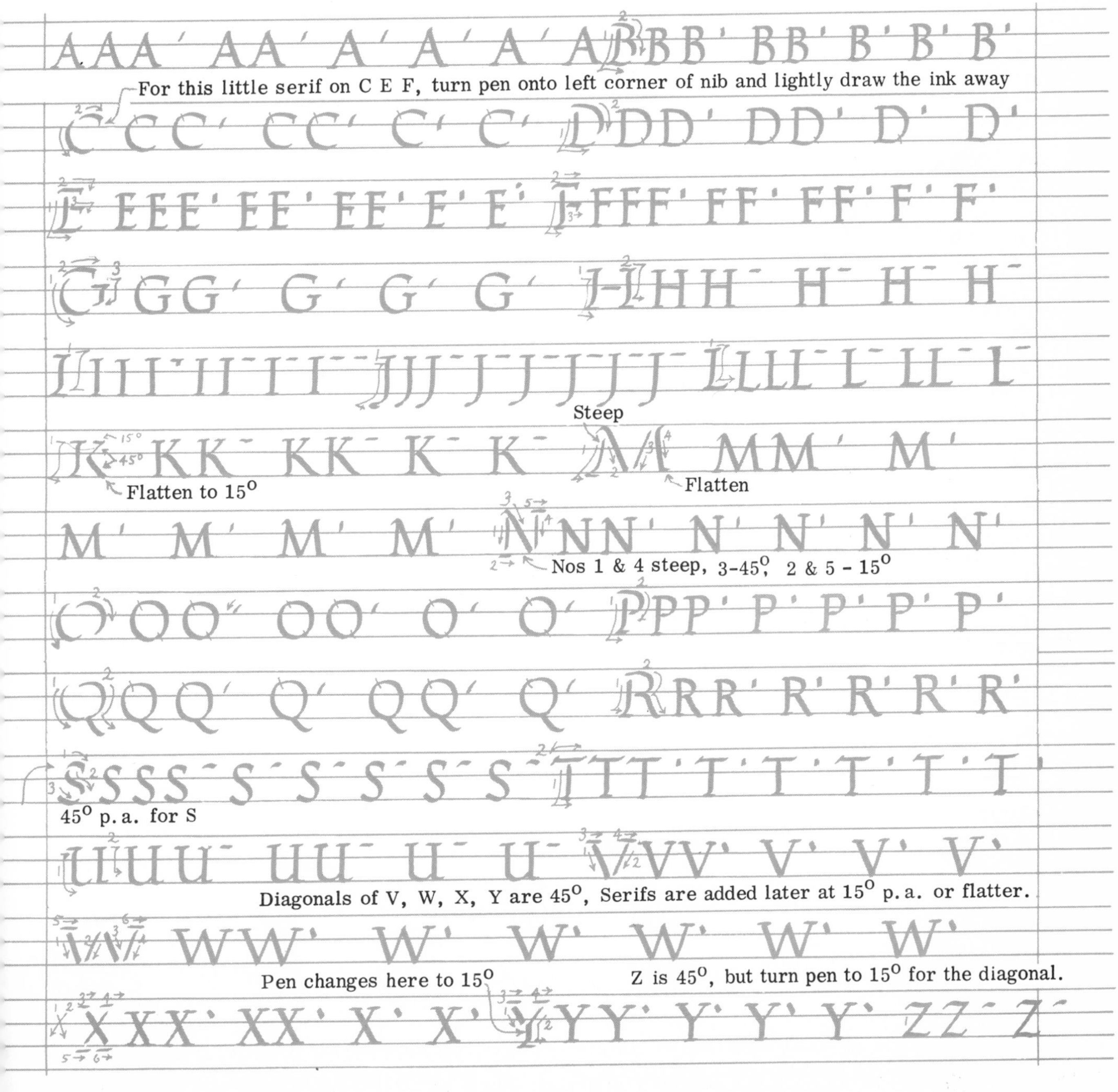

For this little serif on C E F, turn pen onto left corner of nib and lightly draw the ink away
Steep
Flatten to 15°
Flatten
Nos 1 & 4 steep, 3-45°, 2 & 5 - 15°
45° p.a. for S
Diagonals of V, W, X, Y are 45°, Serifs are added later at 15° p.a. or flatter.
Pen changes here to 15°
Z is 45°, but turn pen to 15° for the diagonal.

Jabberwocky

'Twas brillig, and the slithy toves
Did gyre and gimble in the wabe;
All mimsy were the borogoves,
And the mome raths outgrabe

"Beware the Jabberwock, my son!
The jaws that bite, the claws that catch!
Beware the Jubjub bird, and shun
The frumious Bandersnatch!"

He took his vorpal sword in hand:
Long time the manxome foe he sought–
So rested he by the Tumtum tree,
And stood awhile in thought

And as in uffish thought he stood,
The Jabberwock, with eyes of flame,

contd.

LESSON 33: USING ROMAN CAPITALS with the Calligraphic Mode. Use Guide Sheet 4 and copy pages 70 and 71.

Came whiffling through the tulgey wood,
And burbled as it came!

One, two! One, two! And through and through
The vorpal blade went snicker-snack!
He left it dead, and with its head
He went galumphing back

"And hast thou slain the Jabberwock?
Come to my arms, my beamish boy!
O frabjous day! Callooh! Callay!"
He chortled in his joy.

'Twas brillig, and the slithy toves
Did gyre and gimble in the wabe;
All mimsy were the borogoves,
And the mome raths outgrabe

Lewis Carroll

Keeping at it vs. Giving Up

To give up a project because it looks as though you will never succeed in achieving the goal is folly, because it is impossible for you to know how close to the goal you are until you have actually completed the work. It might be the very next instant when all the work you have put into the project will suddenly come into focus and the goal will be won! Or, with a new point gained in your understanding of the work, you will suddenly find all remaining toil much easier.

Once I climbed a mountain in the High Sierras of California, whose side was terraced by nature in gigantic plateaus. Upon reaching a plateau after each gruelling climb, it appeared that the next one would be the top. This continued on and on. I could have given up at any stage, not knowing how close I was to the top. Persevering, I finally reached the summit and was rewarded by a grand view of lakes and plains, shared only by my companion and a woodchuck. The reward was well worth the persistence in rejecting all temptations to give up.

Fred Eager

LESSON 34: USING ROMAN CAPITALS with the Cursive Mode. Use Guide Sheet 5 to copy this page.

Project VIII

DOUBLES AND VARIATIONS FOR BOTH MODES

ON 35: New variations which will work in both Cur-ve and Calligraphic Modes can be used for either slow fast writing, except the variations of b and d, which e used only for speed.

The "tick" serifs shown below would tend to slow e hand, so certainly would not be used for top speed. owever, it cannot be denied that they are really help-ful in "dressing up" a hand, and so they could be used in some compromise between the slowest and fastest handwriting.

TRACE and COPY the material which presents the new variations, give them extra practice on your own paper, using Guide Sheets 3 and 5, then copy page 74 in both modes, using these variations.

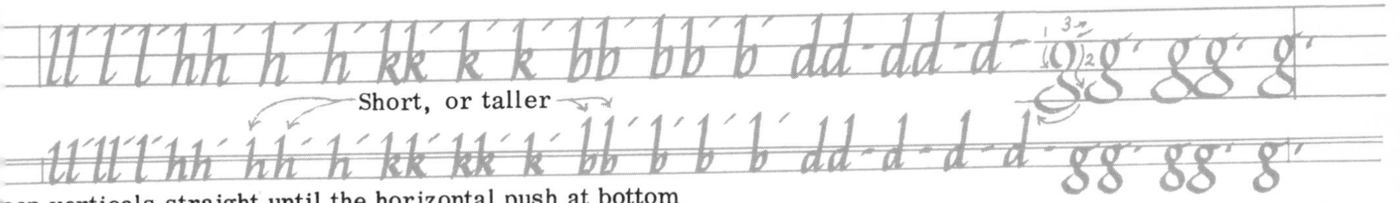

eep verticals straight until the horizontal push at bottom

ne first 2/3 of the tail of q and z is raight. The y descender curves for its length d ends in a horizontal. NOT qu ze Don't touch! and ∂ are for speed only. This form of d used by me Italic writers at the end of words in fast writ-g is not truly Italic, but an Uncial form from the 4th 8th centuries. DO NOT use it after ascender letters.

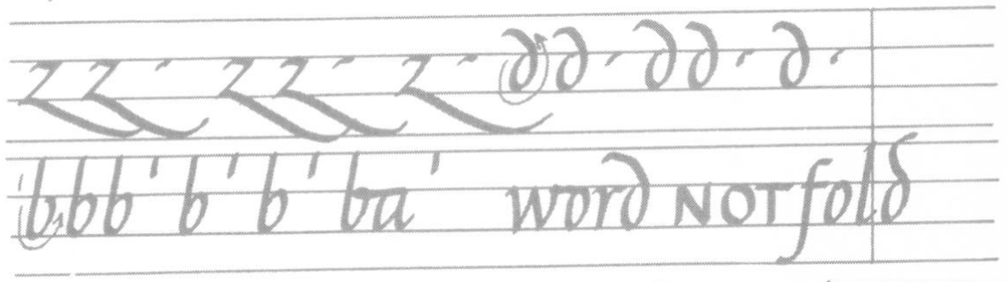

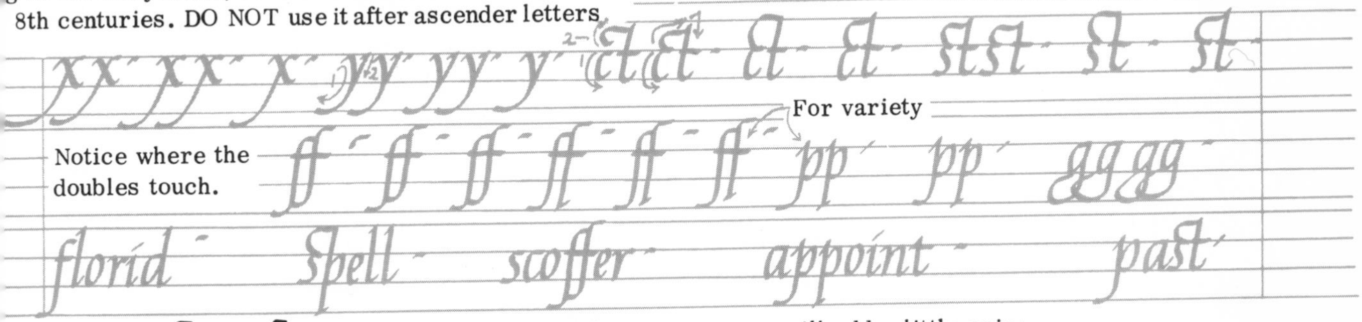

steful use of ct and st, not more than two or three on a page, will add a little spice

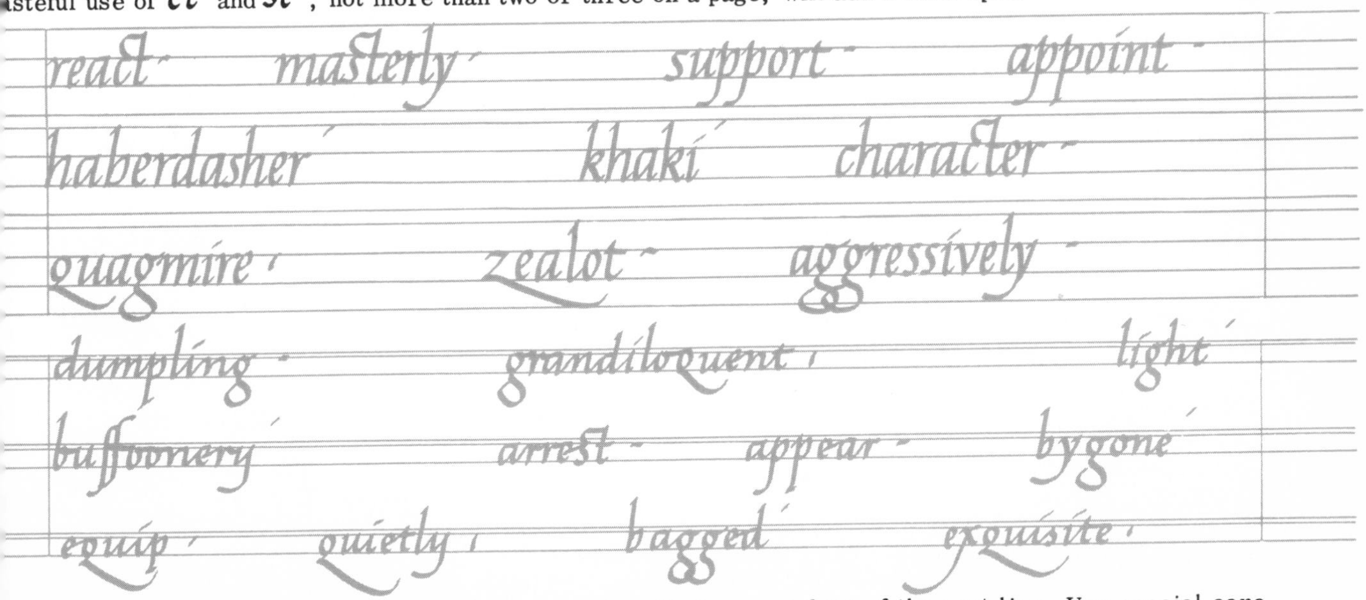

Never allow the descenders of one line to tangle with the ascenders of the next line. Use special care with flourishes. It will help, when flourishing, to space your lines of writing farther apart.

The Arrow and the Song

I shot an arrow into the air,
It fell to earth, I knew not where;
For, so swiftly it flew, the sight
Could not follow it in its flight.

I breathed a song into the air,
It fell to earth, I knew not where;
For who has sight so keen and strong
That it can follow the flight of song?

Long, long afterward, in an oak
I found the arrow, still unbroke;
And the song, from beginning to end,
I found again in the heart of a friend

Henry Wadsworth Longfellow

LESSON 36: Copy this page in each mode, using the new variations.

Project IX

BUILDING SPEED

To lend variety to your practice and to alternate between the rather formal, necessarily slow, careful and unjoined Calligraphic Mode and the freer, faster and joined Cursive Mode, this is a good time to begin exercises toward the development of speed.

LESSON 37: SPEED, FREEDOM AND CONTROL

The following exercises should be practiced three to five times a week and added to the Weekly Minimum Practice outlined on page 65. This practice can be done on a pad of paper you carry around in your pocket or purse for doodling in idle moments. In any case, find five-minute segments regularly for this practice.

1. TIME YOURSELF: To determine your present neat-writing speed, choose an alphabet sentence on page 76. Write it neatly as many times as you can in two minutes. Multiply the number of letters in each sentence by the number of times you wrote the complete sentence; then add the number of letters in your incomplete sentence and divide the total by two. That gives you your present speed in Letters-per-Minute (L.P.M.).
2. DAILY WARM-UP: Now start increasing the speed on each line of your warm-up. Gradually build rhythm and automatic muscular response into your hand. Start each line very slowly and add speed as you cross the line. Don't go so fast that your m, n, and h become spikey and branch too low. You should gradually work into writing freely and efficiently.
3. SINGLE LETTERS: Choose a letter of the alphabet, especially one that you notice seems to break down with speed. Write a full line of the letter, gradually increasing speed as you cross the page. Don't go too fast, but find the rhythm of each letter.
4. WORDS: Choose one word from page 45. Write it slowly, then gradually faster and faster. You might time yourself for l. p. m. on this one word.
5. SENTENCES: Write a sentence or saying from pages 44, 54, 76, or 82; slowly at first, then again, slightly faster, and so on, about four or five times.
6. CHECK YOUR PROGRESS: Repeat No. 1 to see how your speed has increased. If you write 25 l. p. m. now, and can increase your speed by just 5 l. p. m. every week, in 15 weeks you will write 100 l. p. m.

WARNING: Never write so fast that the arches of m, n and h become spikey and branch low. Remember that we read only the top portion of letters in our rapid reading, and the eyes require unambiguous m's, n's, i's and u's in order to call our writing easily readable. If your rapid writing practice is too fast and is too difficult to read, then you are wasting time and are UN-practicing, tearing down when you could be building. SLOW DOWN!

SPEED PRACTICE means, first, gradually building speed while keeping elliptical arches and branching high in m, n, h, k, r; and second, practicing AT the fastest speed at which you can maintain these readable conditions. This kind of practice will keep your writing readable and help you mature a beautiful, rapid, personal handwriting.

You can never expect your rapid handwriting to be completely satisfying. The hand, even when properly trained, will tend to take short-cuts, and these result in deviations from the model. The eye, on the other hand, wants to behold beauty and perfection, and if it has its way will discipline or control the hand until it is satisfied. Thus rapid writing always involves a compromise.

You will find that Italic is less apt to collapse with speed than is the commercial cursive with its loops. The edged pen exerts control over the hand which helps the writing to retain legibility at faster speeds than it would, for example, with a ball point or pencil.

FREEDOM AND CONTROL

Alfred Fairbank, the father of modern Italic Handwriting, writes:

"Control does not imply the writing of a laboured hand that smacks of drawing and excessive precision but rather the attitude of mind that shows determination to write clearly and with grace as well as pace. There are those who prefer so much freedom that legibility is inevitably reduced. They argue that expression of personality has value even when it involves some lack of clarity. Against this plea for expression before function is the more logical one that personality cannot fail to be expressed in good writing as well as in bad if less obtrusively.

"Every mature writer reconciles his freedom and control and decides, if self-consciously, on each occasion, as pen touches paper, how much discipline is to be coupled with how much freedom. More discipline, perhaps, in addressing an envelope, less in the drafting of a letter not to be seen by a second person. The child at a junior school will use much discipline, The adolescent will write with as much speed as he can muster when taking notes and so often in the scramble he must sacrifice clarity and grace. At this stage, periods of careful practice can offset the effects of urgency and dash, and they may be used for the making of manuscript books, with or without decoration and illustration.

"In the Italic hand there is the possibility of writing slowly and with great precision in letter formation to gain a most excellent set script or of writing quickly with rhythmical fluency and free grace."

From page 25 of A HANDWRITING MANUAL, Faber and Faber 1932, 1961, 1966.

WARNING: In writing for speed, DO NOT use push serifs on ascenders which were taught on page 73 because they wreck a rapid hand and tend to become habitual; but you MAY join to ascending strokes with speed, and shorten them somewhat: *hallelujah*

Alphabet Sentences

1. A quick brown fox jumps over the lazy dog. (33 letters)
2. Picking just six quinces, new farmhand proves strong but laz (51)
3. William said that everything about his jacket was in quite good condition except for the zipper. (80)
4. For civilization, Marxist thought just must be quickly replaced by ways of freedom. (69)
5. The vixen jumped quickly on her foe, barking with zeal. (44
6. As we explored the gulf in Zanzibar, we quickly moved closer to the jutting rocks. (66)
7. Joe was pleased with our gift of quail, mink, zebra, and clever oryx. (
8. Travelling beneath the azure sky in our jolly ox-cart, we often hit bumps quite hard. (68)
9. Alfredo just must bring very exciting news to the plaza quickly. (53)
10. If I give you cloth with quartz beads: onyx, jasper, amethyst, keep it. (54)
11. Anxious Al waved back his pa from the zinc quarry just sighted. (
12. Venerable Will played jazz sax 'til 3 o'clock in the morning before he quit. (60)
13. Back home after jiving so, he expired with quizzicality. (46)
14. Adjusting quiver and bow, Zompyc killed the fox. (39)
15. A foxy, quick, clever cat in Switzerland was hit by a fancy sports job with bumpy seats and a grumpy driver. (85)

The above sentences are useful for alphabet practice and speed practice. They also illustrate the use of the two modes with the Cursive Mode in a variety of speeds

Project X

Simple Flourished Capitals

SSON 38: These capitals, like others you are learning, are based on the simple block capitals. The pen angle remains fairly constant, near 45°. *HRW&Y* particularly show how these flourished letter forms are less formal or rigid than the Roman Capitals. Most of these letters are written with fewer strokes so they are very useful in everyday writing. TRACE and COPY one letter, then practice it on separate paper. This will give you more practice on each letter, and save several models of each letter for future review and practice. Now use Guide Sheet 6 and copy the names on your paper.

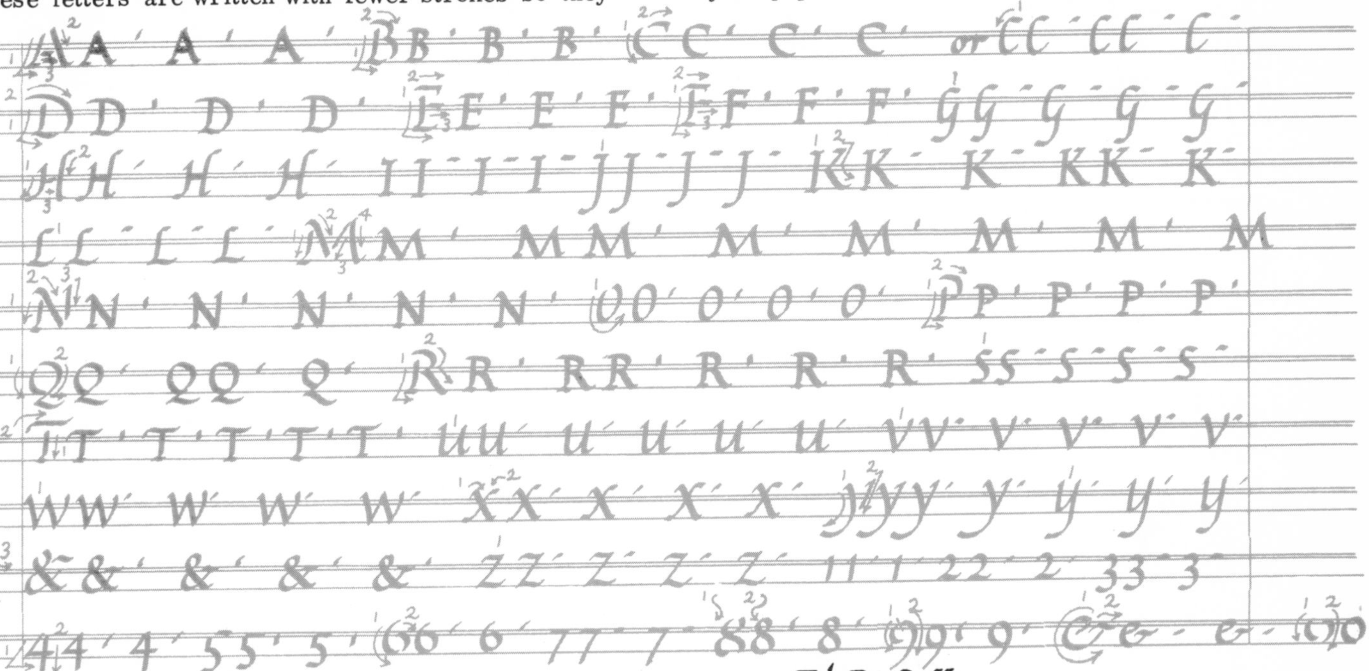

Don't let any letters which follow capitals touch or collide with them *Ed Re Ca Ke*

Keep the size of your capitals between the x-height and ascender height of your minuscules

Autauga Aldrich Bagdad Buckeye Chevak Cordova Desha
Drew Earlimart Edison Flagler Fruita Groton Granby Hockessin
Hosford Irwin Inkom Joliet Jasper Kapaa Kekaha Laurens
Mulvane Morganfield Natchitoches Nobleboro Olney Osterville
Pentwater Quitman Qulin Renville Ronan Scribner Sparks
Tilton Totowa Unadilla Upham Villanueva Valdese Wickliffe
Watonga Xenia Yakima Yankton Zapata Zeoni 1 2 3 4 5 6 7
8 9 10 & & Atmore Bethel Chandler Des Arc Ewa Firebaugh
Guilford Holyoke Ingleside Jessup Kincaid Loogootree Murfreesboro
Narragansett Orofino Payette Quinn River Crossing Randolph
Scotch Plains Ticonderoga Utica Velva Wishek Yeadon
Zelienopole Lost Cabin Beloit Cameron Doty Ettrick Fairfax

Cities & Towns in The United States of America

In the Cursive Mode are you letting the rhythm of the joins at 45° set the spacing?

The Twenty-Third Psalm

The Lord is my shepherd; I shall not want.
He maketh me to lie down in green pastures:
he leadeth me beside the still waters.
He restoreth my soul: he leadeth me in the
paths of righteousness for his name's sake.
Yea, though I walk through the valley of the
shadow of death, I will fear no evil: for thou art
with me; thy rod and thy staff they comfort me.
Thou preparest a table before me in the presence of
mine enemies: thou anointest my head with oil;
my cup runneth over.
Surely goodness and mercy shall follow me
all the days of my life: and I will dwell
in the house of the Lord for ever.

LESSON 39: USING FLOURISHES. Copy page 78 in the Calligraphic Mode, using the flourishes and variations taught on pages 73 and 77. Use Guide Sheet 3 or 4. Copy page 79 in the Cursive Mode with Guide Sheet 6. Notice that the paragraphs on page 79 are marked by "setting out" in the margin instead of by indenting. This way of beginning paragraphs went out of practice as a matter of convenience to printers when movable type was invented. In modern calligraphic (beautiful writing) work, setting-out paragraphs is again gaining vogue and gives the page a nice appearance.

Arrival

We brought up where the anchor was in the chart, about a third of a mile from each shore, the mainland on one side and Skeleton Island on the other. The bottom was clean sand. The plunge of our anchor sent up clouds of birds wheeling and crying over the woods, but in less than a minute they were down again, and all was once more silent.

The place was entirely landlocked, buried in woods, the trees coming right down to the high-water mark, the shores mostly flat and the hilltops standing round at a distance in a sort of amphitheater, one here, one there. Two little rivers, or rather two swamps, emptied out into this pond, as you might call it, and the foliage round that part of the shore had a kind of poisonous brightness. From the ship we could see nothing of the house or stockade, for they were quite buried among trees; and if it had not been for the chart on the companion, we might have been the first that had ever anchored there since the islands arose out of the seas.

from "Treasure Island"

by Robert Louis Stevenson

Are you comfortable writing capitals? Do they look stable? If not, don't despair. Security on capitals is last to develop. Patiently give them regular extra practice.

Project XI

FLOURISHES FOR THE CALLIGRAPHIC MODE ONLY

LESSON 40: Italic writers often enjoy using these push-stroke flourishes on ascenders which may help legibility in a slowly written page. Those who use them in rapid handwriting find that they degenerate into ragged verticals (l l l l l) which play havoc with the appearance of a page. When the slant is even, a page has a wonderful, neat appearance.

Here are three rules:

1. Use the push-stroke flourishes on the ascenders ONLY in slow, careful writing.
2. DON'T use them so much that they become a habi in your fast writing. It is a hard-to-break habit an ruins a rapid hand.
3. DON'T OVERFLOURISH, it's bad taste!

TRACE and COPY this page, then copy page 81 in th Calligraphic Mode, using these flourishes and Guid Sheet 4.

The push stroke must be horizontal as in the beginning of a f s

ll ll l l hh h hh h bb bb b b kk kk k k

dd dd d d ff ff f f ff ff ff ff flfl fl fl

ll ll ll ll fflffl ffl ffl doubles & flourishes

unflagging illumine doodle

calligraphy paleography

fluently illustrate affluent

frostily buffalo philosopher

independently zealous flirt

illustration resplendent hybrid

effulgent emblazon embellish

stultify lexigraphy graphology

quill zealous elfin sprightly

splendor athletic durability

stalwart bulldog quadrangular

OPPORTUNITY

This I beheld, or dreamed it in a dream:
There spread a cloud of dust along the plain;
And underneath the cloud, or in it raged
A furious battle, and men yelled, and sword
Shocked upon swords and shields. A prince's banner
Wavered, then staggered backward, hemmed by foes.
A craven hung along the battle's edge,
And thought, "Had I a sword of keener steel —
That blue blade that the king's son bears, — but this
Blunt thing —!" he snapt and flung it from his hand,
And lowering, crept away and left the field.
Then came the king's son, wounded, sore bestead,
And weaponless, and saw the broken sword,
Hilt-buried in the dry and trodden sand,
And ran and snatched it, and with battle-shout
Lifted afresh he hewed his enemy down,
And saved a great cause that heroic day.

Edward Rowland Sill

ESSON 41: Copy page 81 in the Calligraphic Mode with the new flourishes. Then copy page 82 with half of the passages in the Calligraphic Mode and half in the Cursive.

Sayings of Abraham Lincoln

It is difficult to make a man miserable while he feels he is worthy of himself and claims kindred to the great God who made him.

Let us have faith that right makes might, and in that faith let us to the end dare to do our duty as we understand it.

I am not bound to win, but I am bound to be true. I am not bound to succeed, but I am bound to live up to what light I have. I must stand with anyone that stands right, stand wit him while he is right, and part with him when he goes wrong

I do the very best I know how – the very best I can; and I mean to keep doing so until the end. If the end brings me out all right, what is said against me won't amount to anything. If the end brings me out wrong, ten thousand angels swearing I was right would make no difference.

If you call a tail a leg, how many legs has a dog? Five? No; calling a tail a leg doesn't MAKE it a leg.

You can fool some of the people all of the time and all of the people some of the time; but you can't fool all the people all the time.

Our reliance is in the love of liberty which God has planted in us. Our defense is in the spirit which prizes liberty as the heritage of all men, in all lands everywhere.

LESSON 42: Find a poem and a prose passage you like. Write the poem in the Calligraphic Mode with push serif flourishes on ascenders, and the prose passage in the Cursive Mode with simple tick flourishes.

Making It Yours...

What's Next for You?

A Summary of Remaining Lessons

By now you have built a good foundation in Italic Handwriting. If you keep right on building your hand with what you have learned thus far, you will have a fine handwriting. But for the utmost in pleasure and understanding, you will be interested in the following subjects.

It has been important for your progress that you follow the book this far in consecutive order, page by page. At this point, however, you may select any order for studying the following subjects. For this reason they are listed here with the page numbers, and are briefly summarized so that you may quickly refer to the subject in which you are most interested.

In cases where the instruction is brief, the full lesson is included below. These are marked by an *.

A number of these items have previously been published in issues of Italimuse Italic News. They are included here because they are so important and useful to students.

While you work with these subjects, it is essential that you continue with the Daily Weekly Routine as outlined on page 65.

Project XII: Developing Your Personal Style, or Decisions! Decisions!: Which choices should be made consciously and which should be left for natural development. How to prepare to teach Italic. How to learn. Page 85

LESSON 43: FANCY FLOURISHED CAPITALS 86

LESSON 44: Copying The Prologue by Chaucer 88
Spring by Thoreau

*LESSON 45: FINE PEN AND SMALLER WRITING

Most of the instruction in this book has been on broad and medium pens with reasonably large writing. The purpose of this is to train the eye and hand to recognize and use the correct forms. But as you use Italic writing every day, you may find that a finer pen and smaller writing will suit your hand better, and allow you more speed. This lesson gives you the opportunity to experiment with finer pens.

Some people find that the medium or broad pen is necessary to maintain control in their writing, while others are very successful in using finer pens. Look at samples of writing on pages 96 to 100.

USE THE FINE PEN for your daily warm-up and other weekly assignments (except while working on the Flourished Capital pages).

COPY page 90 with Guide Sheet 6 in the Calligraphic Mode and page 91 with Guide Sheet 8 in the Cursive Mode.

*LESSON 46: LETTER WRITING

Read page 92.

WRITE TWO LETTERS: 1. A newsy letter: a description, for example, of what you have been doing. 2. An opinion letter including reasons backing up what you say supporting or criticizing some action. Also address two envelopes. Study these sample arrangements:

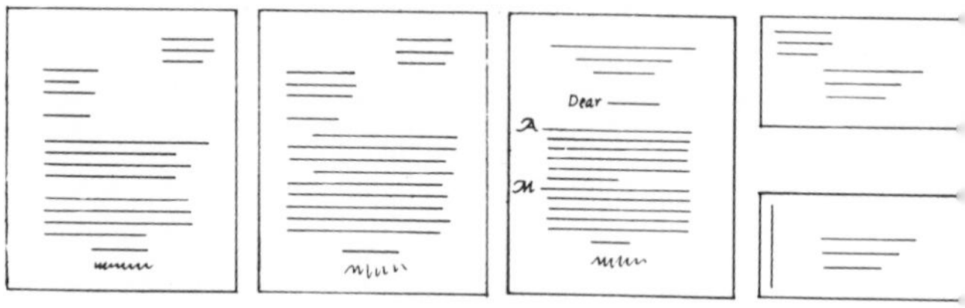

LESSON 47: MORE ON CAPITALS 93

Other uses for capitals to add punch to your writing
1. Letter spacing of capitals
2. Small caps for emphasis
3. Combining Flourished capitals?

LESSON 48: PEN SCALE AND WIDTH OF LETTERS 93

A variety of sizes and weights for your choice.

LESSON 49: COMPROMISES 95

Possible compromises between the Calligraphic and cursive Modes illustrated.

EXAMPLES OF HANDWRITING of Children & Adults 96

*LESSON 50: SIGNATURES

Experiment with your signature. Choose capitals which you like and which are easy to write quickly. They may be capitals you don't use in your regular rapid writing. WARNING! A new signature should be registered with your bank before it is used on checks.

LESSON 51: MAKING GUIDE SHEETS 103

If you want to make yourself a guide sheet with spacing different from the Guide Sheets included in this book, this lesson will be of interest to you.

LESSON 52: DISPENSING WITH GUIDE LINES 103

Now learn how to get along without them!

LESSON 53: THE FIELD OF CALLIGRAPHY & YOU 103

If you have enjoyed working in this book and would like to work more deeply in the field of calligraphy and the historic alphabets, this is for you.

MORE ON MATERIALS FOR ITALIC HANDWRITING

A Calligraphy Student's Library 104
Inks 104
Papers 104
Pens 106

NOTES ON PEN GRINDING by George Miller 105

Spring

The first sparrow of spring! The year beginning with younger hope than ever! The faint silvery warblings heard over the partially bare and moist fields from the bluebird, the song sparrow, and the red-wing, as if the last flakes of winter tinkled as they fell! What at such a times are histories, chronologies, traditions, and all written revelations? The brooks sing carols and glees to the spring. The marsh hawk, sailing low over the meadow, is already seeking the first slimy life that awakes. The sinking sound of melting snow is heard in all dells, and the ice dissolves apace in the ponds. The grass flames up on the hillsides like a spring fire, —"et primitus oritur herba imbribus primoribus evocata," — as if the sun sent forth an inward heat to greet the returning sun; not yellow but green is the color of its flame; the symbol of perpetual youth, the grass-blade, like a long green ribbon, streams from the sod into the summer, checked indeed by the frost, but anon pushing on again, lifting its spear of last year's hay with the fresh life below. It is almost identical with that, for in the growing days of June, when the rills are dry, the grass-blades are their channels, and from year to year the herds drink at this perennial green stream, and the mower draws from it betimes their winter supply. -Henry David Thoreau

Try writing letters and words with your eyes closed. You will be surprised to see how well your hand is learning the sensation of the various letter formations. Give deformed letters extra practice.

Eyecrobatics

Up glance up skyscraper
Soars the body in eyecrobatics
To a bump slide down a bell-tower,
Smooth slide down a curve of concrete
Butter-cream,
A roll down a roof of slate,
Climb up tiled roofs,
Human-fly up brick,
Cat-leap to chimney-pots.
Cartwheels along a sky terrace,
A slithering down window-glass,
Shoot the chute down chrome,
Trapeze-swing ledge to ledge,
Flagpole sitter steeple-jack,
Balancing atop the building blocks,
Tight-rope walking the eaves,
Scaffolds a jungle-gym,
Aerialist of the upward glance,
Scaler of glass mountains,
All in eyecrobatics
Of the city towers

Emilie Glen

Columbus

Behind him lay the gray Azores,
Behind the Gates of Hercules;
Before him not the ghost of shores,
Before him only shoreless seas.
The good mate said: "Now must we pray,
For lo! the very stars are gone.
Brave Admi'rl, speak; what shall I say?"
"Why, say, 'Sail on! sail on! and on!'"

They sailed. They sailed. Then spake the mate:
"This mad sea shows his teeth tonight.
He curls his lip, he lies in wait,
With lifted teeth, as if to bite!
Brave Admi'rl, say but one good word:
What shall we do when hope is gone?"
The words leapt up like a leaping sword:
"Sail on! sail on! sail on! and on!"

Then pale and worn, he kept his deck,
And peered through darkness. Ah, that night
Of all dark nights! And then a speck –
A light! A light! A light! A light!
It grew, a starlit flag unfurled!
It grew to be Time's burst of dawn.
He gained a world; he gave that world
It's grandest lesson: "On! sail on!"

Joaquin Miller

Write a Letter

James T. Mangan

It's only a few steps to the nearest mail box—write a letter! Take a little chunk of your heart and spread it over some paper: it goes, oh, such a long way!

Write a letter to your mother or father, to your sister, brother, sweetheart, loved ones. Are they dear to you? Prove it with a letter! Are they far from you? Bring them near to you with a letter! Write a letter and give them the same thrill you had when you last received that same kind of letter. Think of the joy of opening the mailbox and drawing out a warm envelope enriched with old familiar handwriting! A personal letter—it's good to GET ONE. So SEND ONE—write a letter!

Write a letter to the aged relative who hasn't many days to live, the friend of your father, the friend of your family, the one surviving link between your own present and past. Don't wait for that dear old soul to die till you act. Act now with a message of love to cheer those last few days on earth. Sit down and START WRITING!

Write a letter to the author whose story gave you that delightful half hour last night. Write a letter to the cartoonist whose serial strip you avidly devoured this morning; to the teacher who inspired you twenty years ago; to the doctor who saved your baby's life; to your old employer to show him there was something more between you than a pay check. Be a human being—write a letter!

There's a man in public life you admire, believe in, rave about. Write him a letter of praise, of encouragement. To be "with him in spirit" is not enough—show him your spirit with a letter. We can't all be pioneers, crusaders, presidents—BUT we can help those brave men stay on the track and push through to a grand and glorious success if all we ever say is "Attaboy!" Write an "Attaboy" letter!

Write a letter and—give. Give praise, encouragement, interest, consideration, gratitude. You don't HAVE to give these things; but the real letter is THE ONE YOU DON'T HAVE TO WRITE!

The sweetest, gentlest, and most useful of all the arts—letter writing. Great, grand characters like Washington, Franklin, Lincoln and the greatest men of all nations, have been regular letter writers. Write a letter! Write it with pen, pencil, or typewriter. Use any kind of paper, any kind of spelling or grammar. It doesn't matter how you say it, and it doesn't even matter what you say; its beauty, its GOLD lie in the pure fact that it's a LETTER! Each mistake is another hand-clasp; every blot is a tear of joy.

Do you see a job? Do you smell an order? Is your mind on business? Write a letter. Then write another letter. No business, no individual built on the "write-a-letter" rule ever failed. Because you simply can't fail if you write a letter. Try it, you'll like it. Great joy and many surprises are in store for you. You'll get letters back. You'll get help from unexpected sources. All that you give in your letters will be returned to you a thousand-fold. For a letter is a five-cent investment in bountiful good fortune.

Write a letter! Whether you say: "Attaboy!", "Thanks!", "I love you!", always remember:
A LETTER NEEDS NO EXCUSE!

Mr. Mangan's "Write a Letter" was used by the United States Government to promote the use of the mails back in the days of five-cent first class rates—and is considered one of the four best advertisements ever written.

From a letter to a student: On Letter Writing:

November 15, 19__

Dear Jim,

The weather's been fine. We're going swimming tomorrow. I heard that all the ducks in Alaska are freezing to death! My aunt is enjoying the sun in Texas. Did you hear about the latest rocket flight to Mars? My stars, it's hot now, there ought to be a law! What do you think of the new law passed to make safety belts in baby carriages mandatory?

You see, jumping from topic to topic all in the same paragraph makes the reader feel funny. If you can stay inside the same general subject for several sentences and make a paragraph of it, you will be writing in a manner that appeals to anyone, and you make it easy for anyone to follow.

Try to answer all the questions in a letter you receive the best you can, and see if you can ask a question (not a silly one) that will cause the person you write to want to answer you. Try to comment on other things he says in his letter as if you were talking with him and he had just said them. Show that you are interested in him by the way you talk to him in your writing.

Don't give advice to someone or argue with him until you know him quite well, and when you do, try to be diplomatic, saying it nicely, or leaving a loophole through which he can escape, or you can admit that you MIGHT be wrong. It's funny, but people hate to be insulted or criticized! Because, I suppose, everyone seems to think quite highly of himself, probably because he is the only one he really knows so well. Then to offset this serious part of your letter (argument or advice), have enough chatty, newsy, friendly writing, so he doesn't think you might be picking on him.

What would your pen-pal like to hear about? What have you been doing, or reading, or thinking? Describe something: farm, home, school, town, vacation, city, store, pets, herds, lakes, weather, friends; or anything you are really interested in: write on that with enthusiasm and you are sending a little of yourself in the letter. This kind of writing makes letters important and very enjoyable for both writers.

Sincerely yours,

Fred Eager

SON 47: MORE ON CAPITALS

lways give capitals and numerals plenty of room. Don't crowd them. In fact, they look very well and sort f special when "letter-spaced," i.e. given additional pace between the letters of a word:

HIS SHOULD NEVER BE DONE WITH MINUSCULES *(small letters)*

Simple block capitals may be used the same size as ninuscules for emphasis, instead of underlining words, s in the above all-cap line and in the headings in this GUIDE.

In rapid writing the simple block capitals or simple lourished capitals or even some of the simpler of the ancy flourished capitals on page 86 may be used. But usually the fancy flourished capitals should be used as sparingly as the spices in food.

The use of *FLOURISHED CAPITALS* for entire words is bad, as you can see. Only block or Roman capitals should be used in this way.

The change to flatter pen angle as you write capitals may easily be done; just as the typist presses the cap button for capitals, so you turn the pen slightly. The resulting thicker verticals and thinner horizontals give the capitals stability and elegance.

WORK ON THESE USES OF CAPITALS:

1. Letter spacing of Roman Capitals
2. Letter spacing of block capitals
3. Write a paragraph using "small caps" for emphasis of several words where you might want to use underlining. Use block capitals the same height as the x-height of your minuscules.
4. Write a title line with Flourished Capitals on the first letter of each word, Roman Capitals on the other letters.

SSON 48: PEN SCALE AND SPACING

Study the examples of different pen-scales and different letter widths on the following pages and experiment with some of them. Stick with one combination until you become accustomed to it before going on to another. Your choice of pen scale and width of letters will affect the color of your page, possibly the control of your pen and the readability of your writing.

If you like the Calligraphic Mode, and want a rapid handwriting that is closer to that than to the Cursive Mode, then you must be willing to sacrifice even spacing to some degree, and you must be careful that the vertical strokes are not so dominant, with spikey arches on the tops of m, n, h, b, p, or you will make it difficult for the reader.

You will find that the smaller you write with a broader pen, the more control you will have. The larger you write with a fine pen, the less control you will have. Some people can control a fine pen in rapid writing more easily than others. You must find exactly what suits you best in this respect for your own personal handwriting.

WRITE SEVERAL PAGES experimenting with the different possibilities illustrated here. Find which one suits you best.

Pen-scale is the size of writing you do with a given size of pen, referring specifically to the ratio between the two. It is measured in terms of pen widths, which are determined by the widest stroke possible with your pen. For example, if your pen-scale is 4 pen widths, or 4 p.w., that means that the x-height or body height of your letters is as tall as four pen widths of your pen.

You measure pen widths by turning your pen so that the edge is perpendicular to the line of writing, and making short strokes which show the widest stroke of your pen. Stack these wide strokes to determine your pen scale:

Here is a demonstration of pen scale with various sizes of pens and various pen widths.

Pen Scale:	4-1/2 p.w.	4 p.w.	3-1/2 p.w.	3 p.w.
Pen Size				
Broad	abcdefg	abcdefgh	abcdefgh	abcdefghij
Medium	abcdefghij	abcdefghij	abcdefghij	abcdefghijklm
Fine	abcdefghijkl	abcdefghijklm	abcdefghijklm	abcdefghijklmno
Extra Fine	5⅓ abcdefghijklm	4½ abcdefghijklm	4 abcdefghijklmn	3½ abcdefghijklmno

SPACING AND THE WIDTH OF LETTERS

The spacing and width of letters is measured by two numbers which indicate a ratio of the width of the space between strokes to the x-height of the letters. 1:2 indicates that the distance between strokes is half the distance of the height of the stroke. This distance is measured from the left side of one stroke to the left side of the next.

The author has divided the x-height into five parts and has worked out all the width to height ratios with this constant. Therefore in expressing the ratio of 1 : 2, the author states the ratio as 2-1/2 : 5. This is the spacing set in this book for the Calligraphic Mode.

Arrighi, the author of the first printed handwriting instruction book (1522), uses spacing frequently as close as 2 : 5.

The examples of the Cursive Mode in this book are about as squat (3 pen widths) and as wide (3.7 : 5) as a modern handwriter will find practical. Any smaller and the letters will fill in. Any wider and the hand will have a difficult time making the movements.

Here is an illustration of various spacings at various pen scales.

Pen scale: 4-1/2 p.w. (pen widths)

2:5 Now is the time for all good men to come to the aid of their country.

2½:5 Now is the time for all good men to come to the aid = Calligraphic Mo

3:5 Now is the time for all good men to come to the aid of

3½:5 Now is the time for all good men to come to

3.7:5 Now is the time for all good men to come

Pen scale: 4 p.w.

2:5 Now is the time for all good men to come to the aid of their country.

2½:5 Now is the time for all good men to come to the aid of their country.

3:5 Now is the time for all good men to come to the aid of

3½:5 Now is the time for all good men to come to the

4:5 Now is the time for all good men to come to

Pen scale: 3 p.w.

2:5 Now is the time for all good men to come to the aid of their country.

2½:5 Now is the time for all good men to come to the aid of their country

3:5 Now is the time for all good men to come to the aid of their country

3½:5 Now is the time for all good men to come to the aid of their country

3.7:5 Now is the time for all good men to come to the aid = Cursive Mod

ssON 49: COMPROMISES

Study the examples of handwriting on the following pages, analyze and classify them according to the groups described below.

Now try working out some of these compromises with your own handwriting. See if you can discover what sort of balance in the elements might fit your needs best for a rapid hand. Try using 3-1/2 or 4 pen widths with a variety of widths for spacing.

Copy pages 101 and 102 in various ways.

Of course, at the same time as you are working on this lesson, you should continue developing your slow, careful Italic in a balance of the elements presented in Lesson 48.

amples of Compromises in Italic Hands

On the next few pages are shown some Italic hands of today by children and adults with varying experience from the young student to the master and professional calligrapher.

These samples of writing used by individuals are NOT models to be copied. When a student copies a personal hand, he tends to exaggerate the elements that are accidental departures from a model. This is why a model must be cleansed of all personal idiosyncrasies and be carefully executed. Each writer should have his OWN accidents and not copy those of another.

As a result of your study of Italic Handwriting in the two modes, you will discover that the various hands fit into one of the following groups:

1. Calligraphic Mode—unjoined. Here the writer decides to sacrifice speed in favor of this most beautiful and evenly spaced hand.
2. Calligraphic Mode—joined. Several different tricks make it possible to do this and keep even spacing:
   a. change the pen angle for the joins (steepen it).
   b. force the joins to be steep and thicker. This results from the desire for close even spacing but a determination not to change the pen angle because it would mean slowing down.
3. Compromise—keeping Calligraphic Mode shapes, but joining without changing the pen angle. In this hand even spacing is sacrificed.
4. Compromise—involving more slant (20° to 30°), which also requires a flattening of the pen angle to about 35° to keep the vertical strokes from becoming too thin and scrawny. The pen scale can be the same as in the Cursive Mode (3 p.w.), and still give the illusion of tall letters as in the Calligraphic Mode.
5. Cursive Mode. Here the writing is at a smaller pen scale and the spacing is opened up, making possible a rapid, flowing hand with joins AND even spacing without sacrifice of easy readability.

To judge the readability of any writing, run your eyes quickly along the top of the lines of writing, and see how much of the meaning you can pick up. You will find that your eyes run more comfortably along the tops of writing in group 5.

Two of the scribes are illustrated by more than one letter because they write somewhat differently as mood and time dictate.

ustration of the various groups:

Calligraphic Mode - the ultimate in beauty.

:a *With joins at a steeper pen angle the close spacing is kept*

:b *If joins are pushed up we can get close spacing w/o p.a. change: v*

Here the spacing follows the joins at 45° p.a.

Extreme slant and wide spacing here.

The cursive hand flows very openly & freely with even spacing.

Tweedledum an Tweedledee
Agreed to have a battle,
For Tweedledum said Tweedledee
Had spoiled his nice new rattle.
Just then flew down a monstrous crow,
As black as a tar barrel,
Which frightened both the heroes so,
they quite forgot their quarrel.
Lewis Carrol

Karol Nielsen.

Second Grader (Age 7)

The Wind
One breesy windy day
I went outside to play
And the wind blew my sick away
On that breezy, windy day

On the next breezy windy day
I went outside to play
And the wind almost blew me away
On that breezy, windy day

So for now on a breezy, windy day
I don't go out and play
Because I don't want to be blown away
On a breezy, windy day.

By Nancy Greenfield

Fourth Grader (Age 10)

Before

What helps? There is the table of contents, prlface, author biographies, literary terms, a glossary, a contents list by types and index, the improve your reading sections, the understanding

After

Dear Mr. Eager,
I like Italic Writing because it has improved my writing. My writing used to be very messy. Now it is very beautiful.
It has also improved my personality. I have learned to be patient and keep on trying.
It is also fun seeing the changes in my writing. I am very proud of my writing now.
Sincerely yours,
Susan Lorimer

Seventh Grader

Before

Quick brown fox jumps over a lazy dog.
Quick brown fox jumps over a lazy dog.
Quick brown fox jumps over a lazy dog.

After

The Arrow and the Song

I shot an arrow into the air,
It fell to earth, I knew not where;
For, so swiftly it flew, the sight
Could not follow it in its flight.

I breathed a song into the air,
It fell to earth, I knew not where;
For who has sight so keen and strong
That it can follow the flight of song?

Long, long afterward, in an oak
I found the arrow, still unbroke;
And the song, from beginning to end,
I found again in the heart of a friend.

Henry Wadsworth Longfellow

Sandra Warren Twelfth Grader

Arthur L. Davies · 2401 Chelton Rd. Colorado Springs, Colo.
XX · April · MCMLXXIII
Dear Fred

Why is it that we're all in such a rush? Just making the wherewithal to keep up with the monthly bills takes a rather big slice out of each XXIV hours & now that spring is creeping up on us one can add raking, fertilizing, mowing and other necessary home maintenance chores to the things which keep us from our real pleasures, pens, inks, papers and CALLIGRAPHY! All the above is really just a very long winded.
you sooner.
It was certainly a
you're about t
time go.. good
know about (
people writing
Advertising
that the Peli
New Yorker

2401 Chelton Road
Colorado Springs, Co., 80909
April 7, 1973

Hi Fred:

Thanks for your letter of Mar. 29. I think you are right when you say many people in the Co. Springs and Denver area would like to have italic lessons. I get quite a number of calls from people who would like to find an italic teacher. However, I'm just too interested in doing italic pieces myself to start a class and unfortunately it's only on week-ends that I have the time to "do my own thing". I'd like to learn your secret of time management – you seem to get so darned much accomplished!

I have heard that someone at the "Co. Springs Fine Arts Center" does give lessons in calligraphy from time to time but I don't know his name. I'll try to find out more about it. Meanwhile, it might not be a bad idea to send them a letter and perhaps some info. on supplies. The Art Center now has a new director.. his name is Milo Naeve.

Boy, I do like this new Platignum nib! All best wishes from cold, cold Colorado.. as ever, Art.

43 Ankara Ave. Brookville, Ohio · 45309
August 4th.

Dear Fred,

The visit to Rays was quite an experience. I arrived on the very heels of Don Margo's, Rick Cusick's & the Metzger's departure. Don was there 9 days. The others about 4; all at the same time. Irene was visibly tired as was Ray. So I limited my stay from Tuesday noon to Wednesday afternoon; out of concern for their general well being. Lovely people – Ray and Irene. I've never been in the

43 Ankara Avenue Brookville, Oh. 45309
July 28

Hi Fred – I'm leaving Monday for Ray's. One detour: Harvey wrote and asked me to stop in and pick up the completed copy of his "Visit With RFD" and deliver it to Ray for his observations. So I've changed my whole route to accomodate him. I called Harvey – he was on the golf links – and confirmed my arrival there Monday. And then I called Ray. Don Margo is still there but leaves Sunday. I chatted with Don and Irene for awhile. Rick Cussick plus two others are out there too but in a motel in town. Ray said they're trying to put his books in order. So, I hope to get there early Tuesday morning – I'll leave then on Thursday. I'm anxious to get there – then back. Green beans are now $12.00 per bushel – last year you could get as many bushels as you wanted for $2.00 per bushel. Thats what I call inflation. Food freezers are sold out. Beef is all but gone from most of the local warehouses. So eggs are 89 cents per dozen while chicken is 79¢ per pound. We've frozen all of our vegetables and next week Pat and family will pick and can green beans – free – from friends who have more than they want. I think its going to get much worse as food becomes scarce and prices continue soaring with no end in sight. I've exhausted my faith in politics and Nixonism. I don't believe we will see any developments in a stable economic system until he is out of office. And I voted for him. Depression – Riots – Revolution will be the order of things to be in the future unless some higher force – I hope – takes over. I hate to say it, but what I've always said, is now revealing itself. Dirty business. Well – write. Nobody else has either except Harvey. As ever – Abe

Abraham Lincoln of Brookville, Ohio

Dear Mr. Eager,
Yes, I am becoming much more at ease in my writing, perhaps mostly from having found a comfortable angle of slant to work with. And I am using it more in personal letters.

I wanted to get a note off to you before leaving on vacation next week. Will fly to Denver, pick up my parents, and take them on a flying trip to the midwest. With a partner, I have a very good, fast, and well equiped 4-place airplane, so that is to be our mode of travel, and it is fun. So, with Italic, I have 3 great hobbies, writing, flying, and the game of bridge.

It is interesting to know that you teach music – that was my original career field – had 3 years toward it, then changed to business after WWII, then ended up in the ministry. Knowledge of music has been invaluable to me. Last Sunday saw me as organist!

Richard Willars

Dear Fred,
Thank you for your letter of Jan. 2 and its enclosurers – I enjoy hearing from you about the "Italic" doings in U.S.A. and of course the "Eager" addition to your family – congratulations to you both.

Yes, Fred the Doman Reading is most successful and is still being used for the others – our son has four children now. The address on the set you so kindly helped us to obtain is as follows:– Kiddies Unlimited, Phila. Pa. Ladies Home Journal Dept. J.M.Y. Post Office Box 84 New York 46, New York – by Glenys Doman, George L. Stevens & Reginald C. Orem.

Ken J. Tulloch

(New Zealand)

Dear Fred Eager,
A brief note in reply to your letter of November 4th:

The job on so large a sheet is awe-inspiring to me as I always work so small! At least, you can use a broad pen which I find helps to make beautiful letters.

I get all my parchment from Band & Co. direct (calf-skin MSS vellum) and they give me prompt and excellent ~~ser~~ service, by air mail if necessary, although that is expensive! In New York, The Anderson, Nelson, Whitehead Paper Company, 7 Caight St., carries sheepskin which is not nearly so good to work on. I do not know if they have the MSS vellum as I have avoided their shop for years. They have little interest in their retail customers and give one no opportunity to select the skins personally as they formerly did when it was The Stevens. Nelson Company, and many are defective.

I enclose a little envelope with some Band's pounce, though their skins are already fairly well prepared so I seldom have to use it. The quills I use (chiefly for gilding) I bought in London years ago. I did get some once at the Bindery in

Enid Eder Perkins

Dear Mr Eager,
In writing to ask you for the "Summary of Italic Handwriting" I shall be revealing a very undisciplined Italic hand. I have been at it for some five years and was considerably helped by your "Guide" (which I had from you by mail some two years ago as I recall). The lack of discipline shows up at ~~speed~~ for, though I try to write at least one thing each day with care, I do not sit down with the model before me as I ought and work at the elimination of the many faults. One often has very effusive compliments on Italic but almost

Rutherford Aris

Dear Mr. Eager-
It was a pleasant surprise to hear from you this week. It's been a busy summer and I haven't had time to answer your letter of May 27 regarding the piece for the News Letter about how I got started in Italic writing. I'm not sure that it would be vitally interesting to your readers, but will give you a brief outline to use or not, as you see fit.

I spent the 1st 6 wks. of this summer taking a course in lettering at the Univ. of Wisconsin-Milwaukee – 2½ hrs. a day, Mon thru Fri., in class and another 2 hrs. a day on assignments, reading, etc. As I look back now, I can say without exaggeration that this has been one of the best-spent, most worthwhile summers of my life. After being away from being a college student for some 20-odd years, going back to school was a little frightening at first.

June Morris

Feb. 2, 1972

Dear Mr. Eager:
First of all, let me say congratulations on your new home. I hope you are enjoying your new location.

In my letter to you a year ago I said I wanted to keep you posted on my Italic activities. Since then, I have printed several pieces I have sold, printed wedding invitations and birth announcements and church material for the church we attend. I have designed an Italic display I am going to show at the next arts and crafts bazaar to be held here in two or three months. I hope this will attract several people to request me to print material for them or to let me help them to learn to write Italic. I know I am not experienced enough to be a regular teacher of Italic but I can at least give them information and guidance on where

Farell J. Nokes

Before

Italimuse Inc.

It's me, Robin King. What's the matter? can't you read? Can you guess why I started with Italic handwriting?

After

Italimuse Inc.

Hey, you guys, your idea of a single-page summary is a really good idea!

I have been writing Italic for about 5 years now. I started with Guide to Italic Handwriting, and later bought most of the other materials you offer. I feel that I have a real coördination problem - even with Italic script. You'll see by my "old" hand.

Italic writing has given me a real advantage socially and even at my bank, where I am famous for easy-to-read checks. It may afford me an unfair advantage in courses at the local university.

I would appreciate your comments.

Sincerely,
Robin G. King

Dear Mr. Eager:

I am writing in response to your newsletter which reached me recently.

My study of Italic dates back to a year ago at which time I practiced about an hour a day for several weeks. Since my initial efforts I have neglected my practice sessions and consequently my handwriting has suffered; yet this sample represents a speed of about 130

Roberta Hansen

Dear Mr. Eager:

I have studied and practiced italic for about 4 years, but, frankly, I have not practiced very much in the formal sense. It is a matter of not enough time. Nevertheless, my friends gratify me with unearned praise. Samples of my former script are only available on hospital charts.

I bought my copy of "Guide to Italic Handwriting" at the Princeton University Store about 2 years ago.

Peter Birk, M.D.
2 Crown Terrace
Albany, N.Y. 12209

Ma perche hauemo due sorte dis s come uedi, & dela lunga te ho insegnato,
Resta dire de la piccola, de la qua-
le farai che 'l uoltare
di sotto sia
maggiore che quello
di sopra
si come qui vedi signato
s s s
Incominzandola pure con lo primo tra-
tto grosso e piano chio
tidissi
& ritornando per lo mendesmo idrieto
voltandolo al modo chel sia vno
s
che sintenda

Copy of a page of Arrighi's 1522 Handwriting Manual, "La Operina" by Jennifer Chapman

Italimuse, Inc.
Grand Island, N.Y.

Tallahassee, Florida
15-April, 1971

Dear Mr. Eager—

Although I can't consider myself a really accomplished writer of Italic, I have been doing my best to spread the practice around. I am presently teaching a 10-week course to adults at a local Art Foundation, & I hope to give a course for children in my home this summer. I have been using my own example sheets, & charts & demstrations done on poster board with a home-made felt pen. I do feel a need for more professional teaching aids, though, especially for teaching youngsters. I would like to order a copy of your excellent course, & I would appreciate any further information or advice for a budding Italic teacher. Please send it to:

Anne L. Thomas
1520 High Road
Tallasee, Florida, 32304.

Thank You & Sincerely Yours,
Anne L. Thomas

30 December 1968

To: Fred Eager,

You are requesting information on how long I have studied Italic. I purchased your Guide to Italic Handwriting in April of '67 & practiced for at least 1 hour each day with my left hand (I'm naturally sinistral) After finishing your Guide I purchased your Write Italic & continued my crash program of changing my handwriting. In 2 months I had changed completely to Italic. ¢ I have found that writing with the left hand can be difficult, so in December of '67 I purchased another Guide & practiced with my right hand. Your manual made it easy to change from left to right. This letter is being written with my dexter hand. ¢ Friends & acquaintances comment on how they like Italic hand & I'm always being asked to "print something" for them. ¢ One by-product of my learning Italic is that I now enjoy writing a letter.

Sincerely yours,

Ronald Pendergraft

14 Ap

Dear Mr. Eager,

Your letter was a most pleasant surprise, all the more meaningful to me since I realize just how valuable your time is.

I purchased your Guide to Italic Handwriting, Write Italic, and Introducing Italic Handwriting at a nearby college last August and have been fascinated by calligraphy ever since. Practicing has been a relaxing reprieve from the mundane events of the day. I practice roughly two to three hours at a sitting usually four to five times a week.

A few of my friends recently received materials thru Italimuse at my suggestion and countless others have been enthusiastic, informed of your exceptional books on Italic's instruction.

I have always envisioned myself as an artist of some type, but after college, I began military service and never found the time for formal training; consequently Italics has been my only medium directly involving me with aesthetics

John H. McLain Jr

101 DeWolfe Road
DeWitt, N. Y. 13224
Nov. 2, 1968

Dear Mr. Eager:

In response to your recent circular, I submit the following information and would appreciate receiving a copy of your SUMMARY OF ITALIC HANDWRITING.

I have written Italic for about seven years. I no longer have 'practice' sessions (regrettably), but I use Italic every day. Apart from the sheer esthetic pleasure which it affords, it has been most helpful to me in my selling job, in the preparation of sales presentations, with good results.

Yours truly,

Joe West

HENDRIX COLLEGE
CONWAY, ARKANSAS 72032

Dear Fred
Please forgive my late reply to your april letter I simply forgot it, & please allow me to address you with "just Fred." Enclosed is a partial list of students as you requested.

Next year I am offering Calligraphy only in our winter term (Jan 2 - Mar. 14); however, we register in SEPT. for the entire year. So if you would send me a "bunch" of order forms in late Summer (especially if you anticipate any changes)

I teach Calligraphy as an independent study & last yr. I was inundated with students.

Don Marr

from "Paul Revere's Ride"

Listen my children, and you shall hear
Of the midnight ride of Paul Revere,
On the eighteenth of April, in Seventy-five;
Hardly a man is now alive
Who remembers that famous day and year.
He said to his friend, "If the British march
By land or sea from the town tonight,
Hang a lantern aloft in the belfry arch
Of the North Church tower as a signal light, –
One, if by land, and two, if by sea;
And I on the opposite shore will be,
Ready to ride and spread the alarm
Through every Middlesex village and farm,
For the country folk to be up and to arm."

So through the night rode Paul Revere;
And so through the night went his cry of alarm
To every Middlesex village and farm, –
A cry of defiance and not of fear,
A voice in the darkness, a knock at the door,
And a word that shall echo forevermore!
For, borne on the night-wind of the Past,
Through all our history, to the last,
In the hour of darkness and peril and need,
The people will waken and listen to hear
The hurrying hoof-beats of that steed,
And the midnight message of Paul Revere.

Henry Wadsworth Longfellow

From The Declaration of Independence – July 4, 1776

When in the Course of human events, it becomes necessary for one people to dissolve the political bands which have connected them with another, and to assume among the powers of the earth, the separate and equal station to which the Laws of Nature and of Nature's God entitle them, a decent respect to the opinions of mankind requires that they should declare the causes which impel them to the separation.

We hold these truths to be self-evident, that all men are created equal, that they are endowed by their Creator with certain unalienable Rights, that among these are Life, Liberty and the pursuit of Happiness—That to secure these rights, Governments are instituted among Men, deriving their just powers from the consent of the governed, —That whenever any Form of Government becomes destructive of these ends, it is the Right of the People to alter or to abolish it, and to institute new Government, laying its foundation on such principles and organizing its powers in such form, as to them shall seem most likely to effect their Safety and Happiness.

YOUR COUNTRY

Youngster, let that show you what it is to be without a family, without a home, and without a country... Stick by your family, boy; forget you have a self, while you do everything for them... And for your country, boy, and for that flag, never dream a dream but of serving her as she bids you, though the service carry you through a thousand hells. No matter what happens to you, no matter who flatters you or who abuses you, never look at another flag, never let a night pass but you pray God to bless that flag. Remember, boy, that behind all these men you have to do with, behind officers and Government and people even, there is the Country Herself, your Country, and that you belong to Her as you belong to your own mother. Stand by Her, boy, as you would stand by your mother.

from "The Man Without a Country"
by Edward Everett Hale

SON 51: MAKING GUIDE SHEETS

.fter working on Lessons 45, 48 and 49 you may want ɔ make more guide sheets than are in this book.

On unlined paper, write several lines with the same ize letters and the same spacing between lines that ou want for your guide lines.

Or you may determine the pen scale you want by lacing the edge of the pen perpendicular to the line f writing and making strokes the full width of the pen Fig. 1). Remember that to use these guide lines proprly your letters will overlap them top and bottom.

Fig. 1.

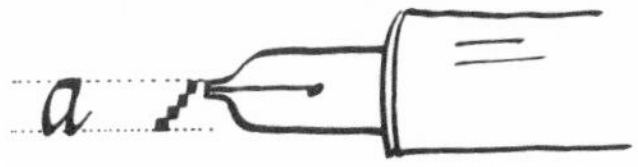

Fig. 2

Fig. 3

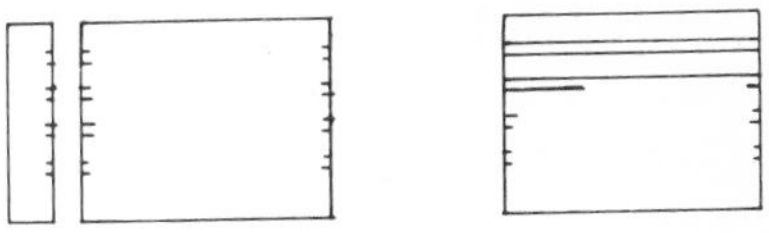

Now to mark your line spacing, set your dividers or the distance between the A lines in Figure 2. "Walk" our dividers up the edge of the paper. Then set them or the distance A-B, the x-height of the letters, and mark this space above each A line. You may also use his same space to mark ascender and descender lines.

If you use the minimum space between the lines of writing (no space between ascenders and descenders), hen you can set dividers at the x-height and mark for evenly spaced lines up the entire edge of the paper.

For drawing the lines, a T-square and board are useful, but you may mark off the lines on the edge of a piece of paper, transfer them to the other side of the guide sheet you are making, then use a ruler to connect them. (Fig. 3.)

Another tool you may find helpful is a ruling pen or a Rapidograph fountain pen designed especially for drawing lines. The ruling pen can be adjusted for different thicknesses of line, but when purchasing the Rapidograph you must choose what size lines you will want to draw. Whichever tool you use it must be used with a T-square or ruler in such a manner that the tip which feeds ink is not in contact with the straight edge and the paper where the two meet, or the ink will make a splotch under the straight edge. Tip your ruling tool at an angle so that the tip is away from the edge. The ink used in your ruling tool should be heavier than fountain pen ink. It may be waterproof or one part of Higgins Engrossing mixed with five parts of Artone Fountain Pen India. But remember to wash your pen after use.

Some calligraphers make different guide lines for each page or calligraphic job they do, using a hard pointed pencil for the lines. Then they leave the guide lines showing. Some adapt standard spacings for certain projects and use one guide sheet, with a light table, for each page.

SSON 52: DISPENSING WITH GUIDE LINES

For handwriting, it is convenient to be able to write straight lines without the use of Guide Sheets. Professor Arnold Bank teaches these three steps: Write OVER single lines first, *like this* ; on another page write UNDER single lines, *like this* ; then on a third page write THROUGH single lines, *like this* . In a fourth way, Professor Lloyd Reynolds teaches students to be conscious of the top edge of the paper as they write the first line of a page, and then use that as a guide for the following lines.

With three pages of lined notebook paper and one page of unlined paper, follow the four steps in dispensing with guide lines.

SSON 53: THE FIELD OF CALLIGRAPHY AND YOU

You have finished this course. You have practiced what you have learned and have developed excellent calligraphic and cursive styles of Italic which are no longer a struggle for you, but seem to flow from your pen almost by habit. You have studied other models of Italic (listed on page 85) and know their strengths and weaknesses. What next?

You might teach others. Start with friends who are surprised and delighted with your new style of writing, and who would like to learn Italic themselves. Get them books, and guide their efforts. When you have achieved some skill in teaching by experience, check with your local YMCA, YWCA, or Adult Education program in the public schools, and set up a course.

You might want to study with a professional calligrapher, and go more deeply into formal Italic, Roman Capitals and Minuscules, Rustic Capitals, Uncials, Black Letter (Gothic or Old English), and other historic calligraphic alphabets.

Or you might want to start the study by yourself. If so, you will find the books listed on the next page helpful.

Most American calligraphers are largely self-taught. To get started they study books, the work of others, and occasionally have an opportunity for a few sessions with a professional calligrapher who guides their progress.

BUT please remember, when you interview or have sessions with a calligrapher, expect to pay for the professional help. It is his livelihood, and time is almost his most precious commodity. It would be most helpful if you would ask him what he charges by the hour. You will find him very helpful and very generous with his time, for calligraphers are a happy lot!

More on Materials

A CALLIGRAPHY STUDENT'S LIBRARY

Here is a list of books helpful to students of calligraphy in approximately progressive order. This does not mean that you should thoroughly finish one before starting the next (You will NEVER "finish" the Johnston WIL!). But this is the order in which you might add them to your library.

Douglass: Calligraphic Lettering
Filby: Calligraphy and Handwriting in America
Johnston: Writing and Illuminating and Lettering
Fairbank: A Book of Scripts
Johnston: Formal Penmanship and Other Papers
Johnston: A Book of Sample Scripts
Anderson: The Art of Written Forms
Two Thousand Years of Calligraphy
Lamb: The Calligrapher's Handbook (often out of print)
Da Boll: Recollections of the Lyceum & Chautauqua Circuits

INKS

For regular writing I recommend Quink. For beginners, especially children, I use Quink washable black and washable blue.

For those connoisseurs who want a really black ink, or a rich brown, I recommend Artone Fountain Pen India and Fountain Pen Sepia. Since these inks carry a solid substance, they will clog the pen unless it is used daily or cleaned frequently. Clogging after short periods of time may be cleared simply by wiping the nib. More severe clogging requires either refilling the pen with fresh ink or soaking the pen nib in water.

Exception: these inks flow freely even after being left for several weeks in the Pelikan pen.

DO NOT use waterproof india ink in fountain pens!

Most fountain pen inks called "permanent" are neither permanent nor waterproof, as you can test by holding your writing with them under a running water faucet. Most of the ink will run off, but a small amount of residue will be left. However, it may be difficult to wash out of clothing.

For calligraphic jobs, for which you want permanence, Higgins India is the standby. But there are a number of inks on the market, and you might try different ones. Of course you would use dip pens with these permanent waterproof inks.

PAPERS

When I test a paper for use with an edged pen, I want three qualities to be present:

1. Thin strokes: //// . On some slick papers these come out too thick. The paper spreads ink, isn't "kind to the thins."
2. Thick strokes: \\\\. Rough papers may cause thick strokes to appear rough along the edges, giving a ragged effect.
3. Friction: There should be just enough tug or resistance so that you can form letters legibly and fast. is hard to control the pen on paper which is too slic but there should not be so much friction that it slo down the writing to a marked degree.

Often an inexpensive bond paper can be found th will meet these qualifications. Local paper supp houses should be asked for samples of paper whi may be found satisfactory. If writers want paper th is a special pleasure to write on, they might try o of the following, which meet these qualifications to remarkable degree. These papers are made in U.S.. and are available at most stationers for handwritin

Strathmore Parchment (Substances 13 & 16)
Crane Fine Line (Substance 16)
Hallmark Finelaid 28L
Crane's Crest Laid (from paper supply houses large sheets).

For more formal uses, the following papers will found of interest, and are available in pads in the sizes: 9x12, 11x14, 14x17, 19x24. Ask for them your local art store:

Strathmore Alexis Layout Paper (16 pound)
Navaho Layout Ledger
Aqua Bee Bristol and Tracing pads
Ermine White Layout and Visualizing Paper

Parchment papers:

Snowflake Parchment (white)
Antique Parchment (golden brown)

Other Strathmore papers available in art stores ma be found of some merit for your use.

Hammermill Duplicator Paper, substance 16 is re commended for regular practice and for letters. Son will enjoy colors in substance 20 for letter-writin This paper is available in pads from Italimuse, Inc.

Xerox paper is very close to the above in qualit but may not be so readily available in 16 pound weigh

One side of most brands of paper is better for wri ing than the other. The difference may be easily dis tinguished in the less expensive papers.

The "felt" side is made smooth by a roller whic presses the paper down on a screen. This is usual the better side for writing.

The "web" side of the paper is that side which toward the screen, and has a criss-cross pattern whic may be seen if you hold the paper at the best focussin distance from your eyes, then tip one side up towar the light so that the paper is almost in line with th light's rays. You will see slight shadows which mak the web pattern visible.

On more expensive papers the difference is not s evident. On less expensive papers, the difference i sometimes such that if you write on the web side yo have a blotter effect—ink spreading through the fiber of the paper. Your pen may catch on these fibers—o at least your thin lines may not come out as crisp an clean as on the felt side.

Continued on page 1

Notes on Pen Grinding

George Miller

First, I'd say, NEVER undertake to grind a nib for anyone else (except at their risk) unless you are more skillful than I am myself! and, at any rate, for first attempts, confine yourself to nibs which are fairly useless—you MAY be successful and produce a nib which will always be a favourite, but you may easily make it into scrap metal! Let me make it quite clear that pens are better left alone when they are writing well, and even a new pen may "write itself in" in a week or two. Pen grinding and sharpening is a last resort—only embarked on when you get to the point of being ready to 'try anything"—You have been warned!

The tools needed are: a very fine carborundum stone (razor-setting type), a sheet of engineer's "Crocus paper," and a jeweler's eyeglass.

Now, here are the three types of pen-points:

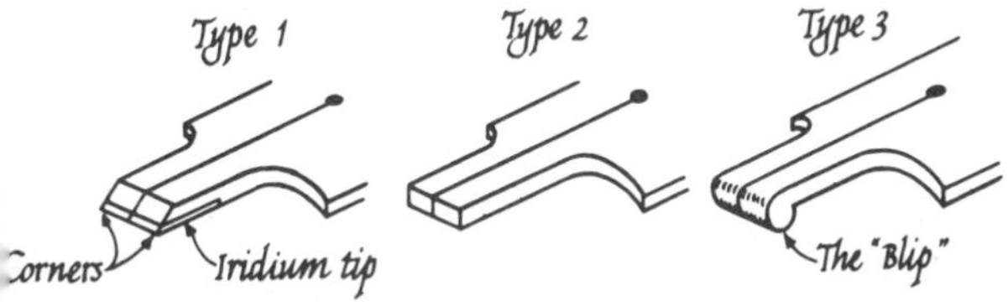

Type 1. Edged pens, are usually of gold, tipped with a harder metal.

Type 2. Stub pens, are usually steel, coated with chrome or brass.

Type 3. Ball-ended pens, may be either gold-tipped or steel-coated.

In case any eye-brows are raised at my inclusion of Type 3, I include these because I know, from experience, they CAN be converted!

Types 1 and 2 are the kinds we usually buy for Italic, so I'll deal with these first, because, more often than not, they need only minor adjustment. When a nib has been used for a while, the bottom may wear so that the edge becomes too sharp and cuts the paper. The following steps can give new life to such a nib.

STUB PENS are fairly simple to sharpen. They need grinding from the top to make the edge as a chisel (like Type 1).

DON'T use oil on the stone—the best lubricant is to wet the nib on the tongue—take the grinding gently, inspecting the edge every 5 or 6 rubs with the eyeglass.

All these nibs, being steel, will cut the paper horribly if made sharp 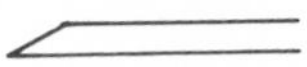 , so when an 'edge' has been ground, one has to round it off very slightly and I have found that the easiest way is to do this on the Crocus paper—mainly by writing on it. The stone always leaves a microscopic 'burr' on the edge—a very thin 'tang' of metal—which has all got to be removed. First, I use (carefully) a sort of backwards and forwards, stropping stroke to slightly round off the edge:

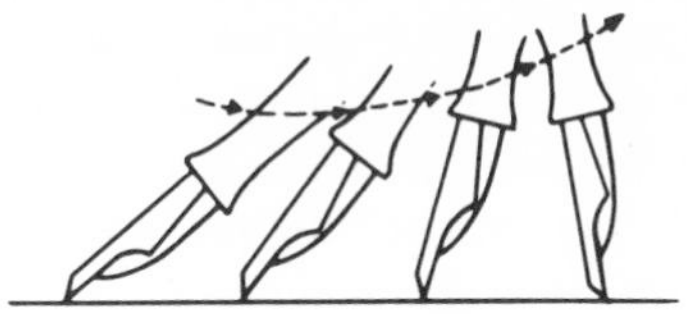

Result: 

and then proceed with a circular movement: , and finally, a little rounding off of the two corners:

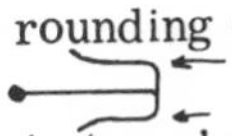

Suppose your pen is too sharp—it catches or jags on the paper, writes roughly and with a brake on speed! Examine it carefully with the glass! Maybe there's a slight 'burr'—a wafer-thin sliver on the edge! Maybe the corners are too sharp—they should be very slightly rounded—to give a 'lead in'—and the edge itself needs the merest trifle of roundness for smooth, speedy writing. In either case, try the Crocus paper first! Place it flat and try writing on it in your normal way, a series of o's. Don't overdo it, and use only your normal pressure, then try it on your paper. Trial and error! A few more strokes on the Crocus—try again! If you suspect the corners, turn the pen onto each corner in turn, and gently rub it on the Crocus. Gently does it—keep trying it on your writing paper.

For the too blunt pen, the one which doesn't show much shading, the stone will have to be resorted to.

If a nib is too broad, it can be made finer by grinding equally from both sides:

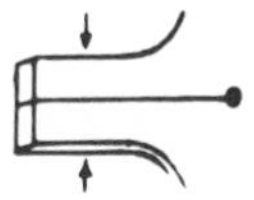

but if only slight "fining is needed, the corners being taken down a little will often be sufficient.

GOLD NIBS. These are rather expensive and are very easily completely ruined. The point to watch very carefully is this: they are ALL tipped with a harder metal, iridium usually (gold would wear too quickly at the edge and be useless) and so, in grinding, one has to be super-careful not to grind away TOO much of this harder material.

If the nib is an 'edged' one, shaped as shown above (Type 1), minor modifications are best done on the gentler Crocus paper, in the manner mentioned above.

With the gold chisel edged nibs, grind only on the bevelled (chamfered) end—turn the pen on its back—use the magnifier—a few rubs on the stone—try it on paper—a few more rubs—try again! Grinding the underside of the nib is a last resort since the harder tip may be very thin! Finally, the nib will take on a new edge, which will probably be a trifle too sharp—this is the time to go over to the Crocus paper. A rub on each corner, a series of loops, gradually you polish off the roughness left by the stone, until with patience and luck you get it writing the way you want it to write. No one else can really do this for you—it is your pen-hold and pen-movements on the Crocus paper which produce the results you need.

Now a word on Type 3 pens! Quite a few of us who go over to Italic writing will be left with a good pen of this sort, often lying unused and forgotten in a drawer! If it has a gold nib—who knows—ground down, it might become your favorite pen, as mine did—if you ruin it, don't blame me!—but if you don't try, you'll never know!

This ordinary type of nib has a 'blip' on the under-side of the nib, and this has to be converted to a 'flat' WITHOUT removing too much of the iridium—giving a profile:  , and then grinding from the top, chisel-edged, to give: 

The iridium may only be about 1/64" thick or less.

I took a chance that most of the 'blip' on mine was of the harder, iridium metal, and ground down the blip to a flat on a coarse stone, leaving still a wedge of the extra thickness. Then I ground the end of the nib back to meet it—forming roughly a 'stub.' Next, I turned the pen onto its back and chamfered it off to a Type 1 shape changing in each operation from coarse stone to the very fine one finishing with final polishing on Crocus paper. I've been writing with it daily for the last four years.

Inexpensive cartridge pens of this type are available and will give you good grinding practice. You may clip off the blip with tin snips, or take it off with a coarse ax stone, then proceed to the finer grinding materials.

I have not attempted to deal in these notes with pens suffering from feed troubles—points which seem to write with only half their width and so on. Such faults are better dealt with at a good pen shop. Have the feed checked first; taking a nib out of the feed and replac-ing it can be very tricky for the amateur.

NOTE: The above article is reprinted from the sec-ond issue of the Committee for Italic Handwriting News-letter with permission of CIH and Mr. Miller.

It is never necessary to grind a pen. However, skill in grinding which will result from a little practice will:

1. Allow the writer to adjust a pen to his touch.
2. Enable one to convert most pens into Italic pens.
3. Increase the useful life of a pen nib.

If a jeweler's glass is difficult to obtain or use, a linen tester or other strong magnifying glass will serve.

If Crocus paper is not easily obtained, a very fine emery polishing paper can be bought at most hardware stores. A coarser paper will work as a fair substitute for the stone.

Continued from page 104

PENS

The Platignum Fountain Pen is a work horse. Very sturdy, almost always ready to flow, and available in a number of sizes for handwriting and lettering.

The Osmiroid Fountain Pen has served well for a number of years, but is more baulky in its flow. For handwriting, though, it is very satisfactory when used with Osmiroid fountain pen ink.

The Pelikan Fountain Pen is a beautifully flowing pen with a more flexible point than the above. It is not yet available in as many sizes as the above pens, but it is always ready to flow, and is a special delight to use.

All of the above pens are equipped with interchange-able nibs. These do wear in time, but are relatively inexpensive to replace. But the nib life can be length-ened if you learn to grind pens. It is a delight to have a pen that gives you crisp thin strokes and still a smooth touch on the paper. See "Notes on Pen Grinding."

DO NOT EVER use waterproof ink in a fountain pen! If you like a black ink that is not waterproof, but it still seems to clog your pen, try it in one of the pens which has a faster flow. Heavy inks cannot be left in fountain pens without use. If you do not plan to use your pen regularly, wash it out after each use, or else keep Quink ink in it. Quink will not clog pens even if left in them for long periods of time.

Dip pens in a larger variety of widths are available in the Mitchell Round Hand pen series, and its Italic series. Both of these are good edged pens for Italic work. The speedball pens are good in the larger sizes (C-2, 1-1/2, 1, O). C-2 is equivalent to the B-4 pen in the above fountain pen lines, and the other numbers are larger.

For pens larger than C-O, you will enjoy the Coit Poster Pens or the Dupont Automatic Pens.

If your pen always skips on the paper, especially at the bottom of pages, use a cardboard or folded piece of paper under your hand while you write. Oil from your hand is probably penetrating the paper and mak-ing it impregnable to your ink. Some papers are more prone to this problem than others.

In the summer, if you are perspiring freely, you should also protect the paper from your hand in the same manner as above.

OTHER WRITING TOOLS

One who has mastered Italic will be able to write bet-ter with other tools than before that study. Some writ-ers have better control of their hands than others. For these the wayward ball point pen may be useful. But the ball point in no way helps control the hand. A 2B pencil is better because there is more friction, but the best tool other than an Italic pen is the nylon-tipped pen. Re-quiring no pressure and yet a degree of friction, avail-able in a riot of colors, this tool is plain fun to use.

But nothing can compare with the Italic edged pen. Children should not use other tools until they have gained a degree of freedom and speed with an Italic pen.

Buoys...

How to Use the Guide Sheets

Each Guide Sheet is marked to indicate the pen to be used and the pen-scale for that size pen. B:4-1/2 means that the ruling will give you a pen scale of 4-1/2 pen widths for the x-height of your letters when written with a Broad pen.

The "x-height" is the primary body height of the lower-case alphabet and is identical to the height of the letters a, n, x, etc.

Some Guide Sheets may be used with more than one choice of distance between the lines of writing. This distance is called "interlinear spacing."

The number of lines on each guide sheet is given to help you find which sheet will fit the poem you copy.

41 different combinations of pen size, pen scale, and interlinear spacing are possible on these Guide Sheets.

For example, on No. 1a you use the Broad pen at a pen scale of 4-1/2 with an interlinear spacing of 3 x-heights by writing on the lines marked by the arrows. When you turn the sheet around you have No. 1b, on which you use the same pen with the same pen sca[l] but with an interlinear spacing of 2 x-heights.

On No. 5 you have a choice of three sizes of pe[n] with two pen scales for each, depending on whether y[ou] use the smaller or larger space for the x-height [of] your letters.

No. 8 is ruled so that you may write in two colum[ns] if you choose, with three choices of interlinear spacin[g].

REMEMBER:

Make the curves and points of your letters slight[ly] overlap the guide lines.

A pen scale of 4-1/2 is for the Calligraphic Mode [of] Italic Handwriting.

A pen scale of 3 is for the Cursive Mode.

Anything in between is for various compromise[s] between the two.

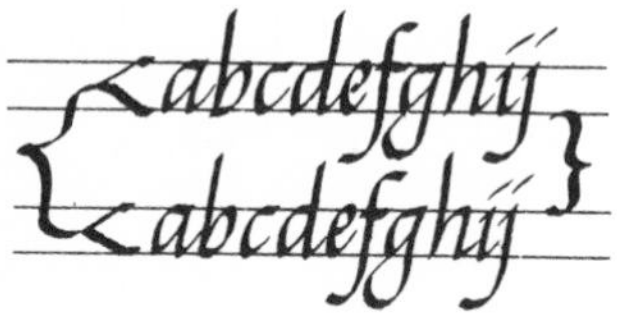

LIST OF GUIDE SHEETS		No. of Lines
1	B:4-1/2 pen widths	12 or 15
2	B:3; M:4; FM 4-1/2	18
3	M:4-1/2	17
4	M:4-1/2	20
5	M:3, 3-1/2; F:3-3/4, 4-1/2; FM:3-1/3 or 4	20
6	M:3, 3-1/2; F:3-3/4, 4-1/2; FM:3-1/3 or 4	28
7	F:3-1/3, 4; XF:4-1/2, 5-1/3; FM3, 3-1/2	26
8	F:3; XF:4	21, 32, or 41
9	M:3-1/2; F:4-1/2; FM: 4	25
10	F:4; XF:5-1/2; FM:3-1/2	29
11	F:3-1/2; XF:4-1/2; FM:3	32

CLASSIFICATION OF GUIDE SHEETS BY PEN SIZE				
Pen Nib	Abbreviation	Pen Scale	Guide Sheet No.	No. of Lines
Broad	B	4-1/2 3	1 2	12, 15 18
Medium	M	4-1/2 4-1/2 4 3, 3-1/2 3-1/2 3, 3-1/2	3 4 2 5 9 6	17 20, 15 13 20 25 28
*Fine-inter-Medium	FM	4-1/2 3-1/3, 4 4 3-1/3, 4 3, 3-1/2 3-1/2 3	2 5 9 6 7 10 11	18 20 25 28 26 29 32
Fine	F	3-3/4, 4-1/2 4-1/2 3-3/4, 4-1/2 3-1/3, 4 4 3-1/2 3	5 9 6 7 10 11 8	20 25 28 26 29 32 21, 32, 41
Extra Fine	XF	4-1/2, 5-1/3 5-1/2 4-1/2 4	7 10 11 8	26 29 32 21, 32, 41

*The Fine-inter-Medium pen is not yet available in the Platignum line

CHECK LIST + WRITING RECORD + SELF EVALUATION

NAME / Other Comments																						
Neat Papers																						
Carefulness																						
Spacing																						
Joins																						
Serifs																						
Alignment (Size)																						
Slant																						
Capitals																						
v, w, x, y, z																						
f, t, s																						
b, p																						
m, n, h, k, r																						
o, c, e																						
a, d, g, q, u																						
Pen Angle																						
Self-grading of one page																						
Speed Work (after page 64)																						
No. pages of School Work																						
No. of Poems																						
No. pages of Assigned Work																						
Extra Practice on Faults																						
Daily Warm-up																						
Weekly Alphabet																						
GRADE II																						
GRADE I																						
DATE																						

for one week. Final grade is average of I & II

CHECK LIST + WRITING RECORD + SELF EVALUATION

Each line is for one week. Final grade is average of I + II

I Marking: 1 (no. of pages); 0 (this item missing)
Grading: No item missing = A. 1 missing = B
2 - C. 3 - D. 4 - E. 5 - F.

II Marking: Excellent = +, Average = blank, Needs extra work = ✓
Grading: No faults = A+, 1 fault = A, 2 = B+, 3 = B, 4 = C, 5 = D, 6 = E, 7 = F

DATE	GRADE I	GRADE II	Weekly Alphabet	Daily Warm-up	Extra Practice on Faults	No. pages of Assigned Work	No. of Poems	No. pages of School Work	Speed Work (after page 64)	Self-grading of one page	Pen Angle	a, d, g, q, u	o, c, e	m, n, h, k, r	b, p	f, t, s	v, w, x, y, z	Capitals	Slant	Alignment (size)	Serifs	Joins	Spacing	Carefulness	Neat Papers	NAME / Other Comments

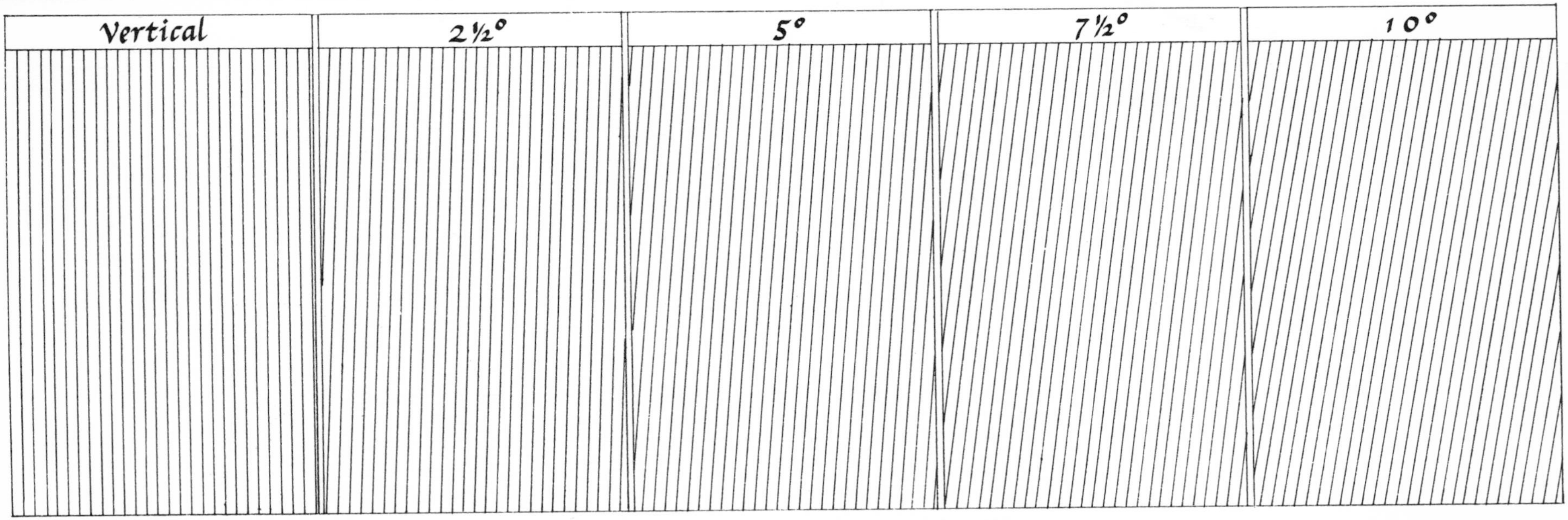

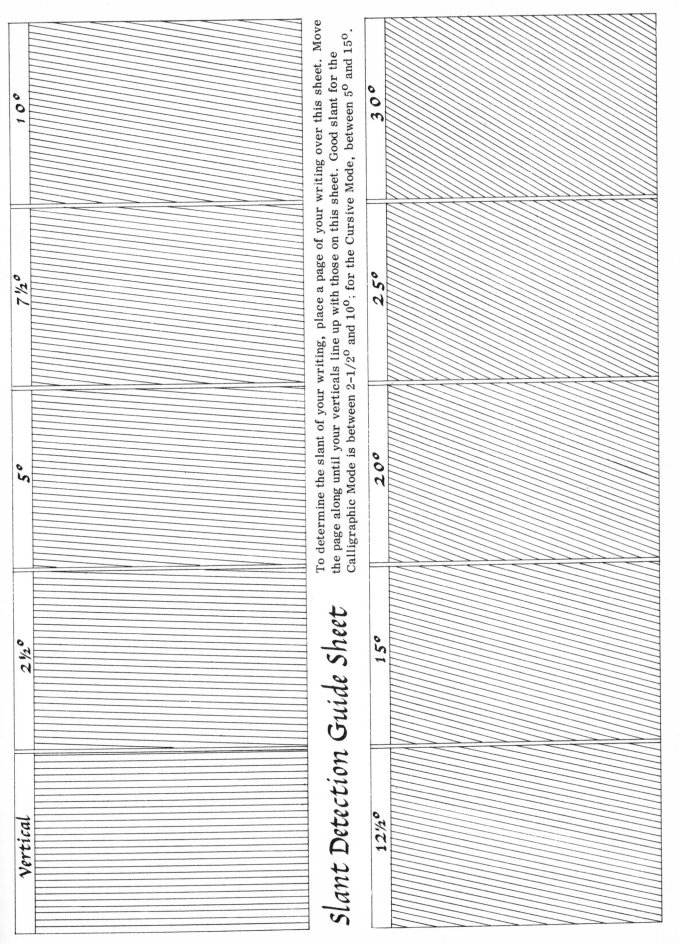

Slant Detection Guide Sheet

To determine the slant of your writing, place a page of your writing over this sheet. Move the page along until your verticals line up with those on this sheet. Good slant for the Calligraphic Mode is between 2-1/2° and 10°; for the Cursive Mode, between 5° and 15°.

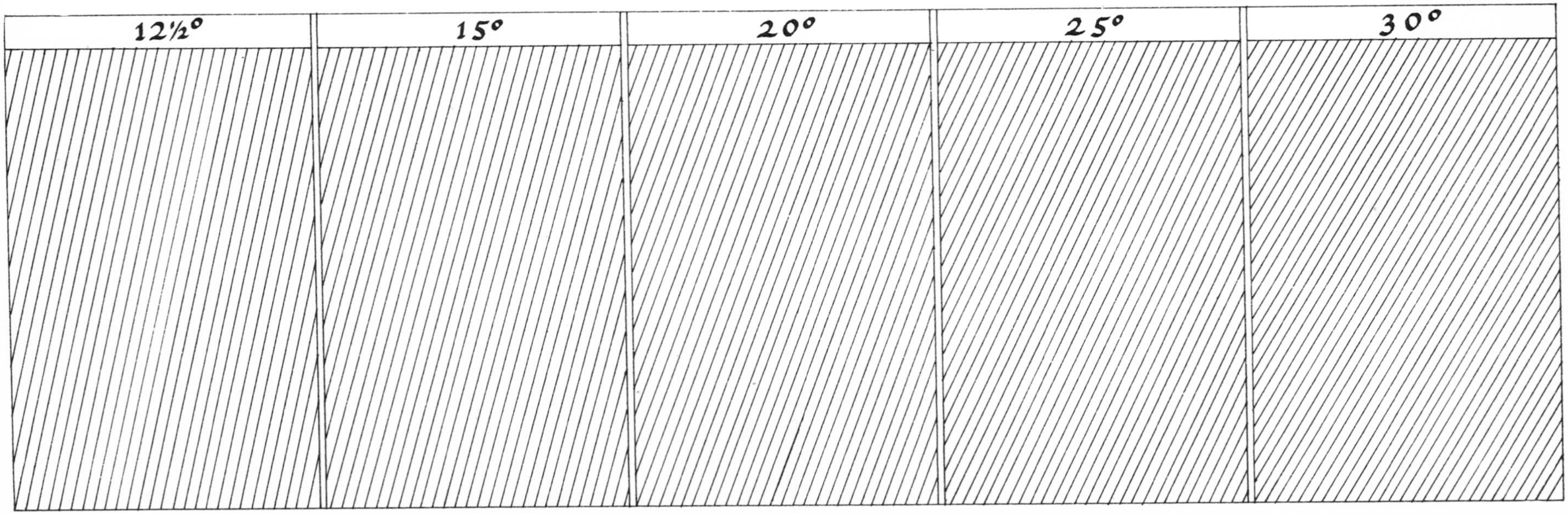

Daily Warm-up of ____________________

NAME

First Day Date: ____________

1

2

3

4

5

6

Second Day Date: ____________

1

2

3

4

5

6

Third Day Date: ____________

1

2

3

4

Third Day, continued

5

6

Fourth Day Date: ____________

1

2

3

4

5

6

Fifth Day Date: ____________

1

2

3

4

5

6

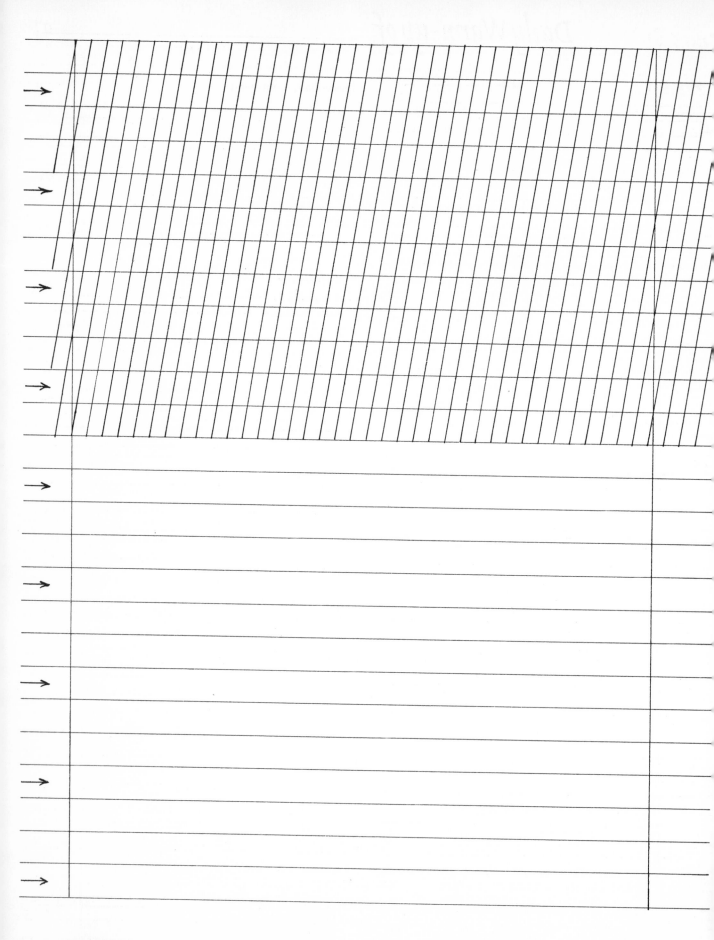

L *Nylon-tip pens for spacing study*

16

15 Lines

1a B : 4½ penwidths

12 Lines

2 B: 3 ; M: 4 ; FM: 4½

18 Lines

17 Lines

15 Lines

4a M : 4½

20 Line

M : 3 or 3½ ; F : 3¾ or 4½ ; FM : 3⅓ or 4

20 Lines

6 M : 3 or 3½ ; F : 3¾ or 4½; FM : 3⅓ or 4

28 Lin

 F: 3⅓ or 4; XF: 4½ or 5⅓; FM: 3 or 3½

26 Lines

Use every line with an arrow, or use lines with long arrows only

41 or 21 Lines

8a F:3 ; XF:4 *Use inside margins; or for 2 columns, outside margins & gutter* 32 Lines

9 M:3½; F:4½; FM:4 25 Lines

10 F: 4; FM 3½; XF 5½ 29 Lines

1 F: 3½ ; FM: 3 ; XF: 4½

32 *Lines*